The Failure Files

perspectives on failure

Edited by David Hillson

Published in this edition in 2011 by:
Triarchy Press
Station Offices
Axminster
Devon. EX13 5PF
United Kingdom

+44 (0)1297 631456
info@triarchypress.com
www.triarchypress.com

A catalogue record for this book is available from the British Library.

Cover design by Heather Fallows -
www.whitespacegallery.org.uk

ISBN: 978-1-908009-30-2

About Triarchy Press

Triarchy Press is an independent publishing house that looks at how organisations work and how to make them work better. We present challenging perspectives on organisations in pithy, but rigorously argued, books.

For more information about Triarchy Press, or to order any of our publications, please visit our website or drop us a line:

www.triarchypress.com

We're now on Twitter: @TriarchyPress

and Facebook: www.facebook.com/triarchypress

CONTENTS

LIST OF FIGURES

EDITOR'S PREFACE:
THE GLORY OF FAILURE

David Hillson

Failure. We've all done it. Some fail gradually, others fail grudgingly and occasionally people fail graciously. But is it really possible to fail gloriously?

The term 'Glorious Failure' has a certain ring to it, and perhaps that's what has attracted people to the RSA 'Glory of Failure' project since it was first suggested by Mitch Sava in April 2008 (and it wasn't an 'April Fool' hoax – I checked). Since then a small but committed group has explored the topic from a wide range of angles, looking for ways to understand what it might mean to fail gloriously. The link with the RSA ensured that our endeavours included societal and transformational dimensions, but the project soon acquired a life of its own.

Following a successful First Failure Colloquium in September 2009, it was clear that we were on to something. Speakers at that event shared their ideas and insights on failure in a variety of settings, and those present realised they were hearing a message that was quite unique and special. From that realisation *The Failure Files* was born.

This book does not pretend to be exhaustive or comprehensive on the subject of failure. Instead it reports our work-in-progress, presenting an array of essays on how failure might be encountered in different ways. Part One sets the scene, with an opening chapter from Mitch Sava and Jonathan Jewell who launched the 'Glory of Failure' project. They describe the thinking and vision behind the project, explaining why failure is an important topic and how understanding failure can transform individuals, organisations and society. A second chapter completes Part One by offering a structured framework for failure, relating it to success, suggesting some defining characteristics and proposing a typology of failure.

The main body of *The Failure Files* is in Part Two, where experts and practitioners from various professions and industries discuss failure in their area of expertise, presenting illustrative case studies and examples, and highlighting the specific nature of failure in their setting. This is where the book's subtitle is relevant: Perspectives on Failure. Each chapter in Part Two offers a unique view of failure from a specific angle, yet together they provide a rich description of the landscape. My goal as editor was to preserve each author's voice, merely performing a 'light edit' rather than imposing a common 'house style'. As a result the Part Two chapters are all different, approaching the topic in the way that each author felt was appropriate. I'm grateful to authors for offering their insights freely, and for trusting their material to my editorial scrutiny.

Of course Part Two could have been a great deal longer, including perspectives on many other different types of failure, or multiple perspectives on each failure domain. As editor I am aware of what didn't make it into this book, but I remain confident that the material here offers the reader much food for thought and action. The disparate strands of our individual authors are, however, synthesised as the book closes in Part Three, with a final chapter that compares the insights in Part Two with the vision in Part One, identifying the next steps and remaining work for the 'Glory of Failure' project. We hope to leave readers with a clear impression of the direction and momentum of activity, as well as an indication of how those who are interested might get involved. *The Failure Files* close with a call to arms, encouraging each one of us to engage positively with failure wherever it is encountered and to seek transformational responses at every level.

This reminds me of a well-known motivational poster which tells us that 'We can't make SUCCESS without U.' In the same vein, I have also realised that 'Making FAILURE requires both U and I.' I hope that you will find much to challenge and inspire you in *The Failure Files*, and that all your future failures will be glorious.

© David Hillson

PART 1

CHAPTER 1:
CONTEXTS FOR FAILURE

Mitch Sava & Jonathan Jewell

UK society has long been seen to be characterised by a pervasive **fear of failure**. But to shield ourselves from failure is to deny ourselves the fruits of our creative and innovative potential. It also makes life boring.

WHY FAILURE?

We like and need innovation

Change is part of life. Sometimes we eagerly anticipate change; perhaps more often we look upon it with hesitation. But there is no way to avoid change; it is not only a constant aspect in our world, but a crucial one.

In many areas of our life, the status quo is unsustainable. We face challenges small and large across many fronts: economic, business, social, environmental, etc. For many of these, the simple, low-risk tweaks of which we are so fond are simply not up to the task. Solving the big challenges will require bold thinking and new ideas. Or, using another word that is popular at the moment: innovation.

Innovation and failure go hand-in-hand

Innovation, however, cannot exist without the risk of failure. When we try new things, sometimes they just don't work. Failure is a natural by-product of innovation. If we are to succeed in developing and exploiting new ideas, we must be prepared – emotionally, financially, socially – to encounter the inevitable failures that will line our path. In striving for greater achievement, a healthy attitude towards failure and uncertainty is considered *vital* to an individual's and an organisation's capacity to create and to innovate.

It is no surprise then that our most successful individuals and organisations are those that are the most tolerant of failure. One apparent constant amongst such people and enterprises is that when asked to identify their most significant failure in life, they do not hesitate to answer. All have encountered some misstep or obstacle along their path that had less than the desired outcome. However, they will also quickly note that it was because of such failures, rather than despite them, that they were able to achieve greatness. Rather than being destroyed by adversity and setbacks, they learned from them. To borrow a phrase from management guru Warren Bennis, these were 'crucible moments' in which their character was transformed, emerging stronger and more resilient than before. Failure teaches us how to do things better, how to adapt to change and the unexpected, and ultimately entices us to reach further.

Failure is in the eye of the beholder

For our highest achievers and for those that actively court new ideas and explore new ventures, setbacks are viewed as a natural part of the process – so natural and anticipated that they are unlikely to be seen as 'failures'. The bar for what defines 'failure' is set much higher.

Failure is considered to be an essential part of building a successful business, or making that breakthrough discovery. In the United States, many venture capitalists actively seek demonstrations of past failure in their prospective entrepreneurs as evidence of personal sacrifice and valuable life learning. This 'School of Hard Knocks' is perceived to be as valuable as a Harvard MBA. Penn State University even has a course for engineering students called Failure 101, encouraging experimentation and radical creativity.

Despite this, there continues to be a pervasive fear of failure

Perhaps one of the most oft cited, although poorly researched, cultural challenges facing the United Kingdom is the population's alleged fear of failure. In the 2009 UK Global Entrepreneurship Monitor Report, 36% of respondents indicated that the fear of failure would prevent them from starting a business, compared with 21% in the United States. While this statistic relates to only one of the UK's policy objectives (increasing rates of entrepreneurship), it is often used as a proxy of a negative public attitude towards failure. This is bolstered by anecdotal evidence, characterised in speeches by prominent politicians, entrepreneurs, and educators, that paints a picture of the UK as a nation of the risk-averse, its ambition to be a dominant and growing knowledge economy held back by an ethereal fear of failure.

In some ways this fear is justified

This is not to imply that we should have a flippant attitude towards failure. In some fields, such as public health or the provision of social services, failure can have very real and drastic consequences. As recent times have shown us, failure in business can have massive environmental and social impacts spreading far beyond their initial domain.

We must all embrace the glory of failure

Nonetheless, without an appetite for experimentation and creation – and the capacity to absorb the occasional failure that inevitably accompanies trying something new – we deny ourselves the joy of accomplishment and discovery, as well as the resulting benefits for ourselves and society.

We must have a healthy respect for failure, in the same way we might have for other powerful forces of nature. And, as with those forces, we should be willing to harness that power to achieve more for our society.

ABOUT THIS PROJECT

When the Royal Society for the encouragement of Arts, Manufactures and Commerce (RSA) was established over 250 years ago it was conceived as 'a cradle of enlightenment thinking'. Today the RSA is a powerful force for social progress, committed to removing the barriers to that progress. What could be a larger barrier to such progress than a fear of failure?

What makes the RSA unique amongst chartered organisations is the multidisciplinary nature of its remit and its Fellowship. The RSA and its Fellows combine research and policy development with, vitally, practical action. Additionally, with political independence, it is not bound by party allegiance or ideology, and Fellows are free to think, experiment, and – of course – to fail. RSA Fellows are encouraged to initiate projects in which to pursue their own ideas and, in so doing, to further the aims and ideals of the RSA. Out of this context 'The Glory of Failure' project was born, starting with a simple article in the RSA Journal ('The Joy Of Failure', *RSA Journal*, Spring 2008 issue) inviting Fellows to express an interest in this fascinating and important topic.

The Glory of Failure project started with a hypothesis: *Failure, at its heart, is a personal thing.* By shining light on the stories of those people who have experienced failure and emerged stronger for that experience, we might, in our own small way, be able to chip away at our collective fear of failure.

Like all RSA projects, the Glory of Failure hopes to generate new models for tackling social, organisational, educational, and individual challenges of the day. And with a 27,000-strong Fellowship of free thinkers, social innovators, and practitioners, we could certainly think of no better organisation to face our fear of failure head-on.

Viewing failure from several perspectives

In September 2009, under the auspices of the RSA Networks programme, we hosted the First Failure Colloquium in London, which brought together a range of interested people (all of whom were leaders in their respective fields) to speak about failure from different perspectives. These ranged from the academic and theoretical to highly personal stories of individual or organisational failure.

The notion was to bring people together to thrash out elements of failure that related across these diverse fields. What resulted was much discussion about principles of failure, dimensions of failure, sectors of failure, levels of failure, and more opinions than people in the room. Despite the complexity of the issue and the range of perspectives, what became clear to all was the unifying nature of the subject. The First Failure Colloquium proved to be a unique opportunity to bring together some disparate groups of people to discuss a topic that is common to us all: the experience of failure and learning from it – or not.

ABOUT THIS BOOK

As the presentations and debate progressed throughout the day, one particular thought occurred independently to several in the room: 'We're really on to something here'. The impressive depth of the content and ideas, both from the presenters and the participants, ultimately led to what you now have in your hands: *The Failure Files* book. From the starting point of the First Failure Colloquium, a solid basis for more rigorous analysis and action has emerged.

In addition to working on *The Failure Files* book, we decided to build a repository of stories where people can relate to aspects of failure and start to challenge its taboo status. Initial anecdotes were refined and extended through a series of online discussions catalysed by a set of simple questions:

- Give an example of your experience of failure.
- How did you respond to this failure?
- How did you learn from this failure and how has it helped you?
- There's a difference between experiencing failure and being a failure, why is this?
- What would you recommend to other people facing a similar situation?

Three personal stories of failure based on these questions are given below. As you read through this book, try to answer these questions yourself and see if it helps you think about failure in a new way. There is no right and wrong. After all, this is about failure.

One of the funny things about failure is that it all seems to come at once. **Jonathan Jewell** *provides an example of failure that was simultaneously a business experience and personal.*

1. **My experience of failure.** I decided to start out in consultancy working with my best friend and colleague from a previous job. Within a year (which actually started very successfully) we had got into the very serious position of a relationship breakdown between us that eventually undermined the company and destroyed our friendship.

2. **How I responded to this failure.** I ended up in a highly contradictory phase where we were trying to wind up the company in a professional manner and, at the same time, dealing with an acrimonious relationship where great care and concern for each other had existed before. I acquiesced on money in a desperate attempt to preserve the friendship but I underestimated the damage that had been caused. When I realised that only I was trying to save 'us', I had moved into a state where I saw him as greedy and unscrupulous. It took a long time to get over.

---

3. **What I learned from this failure.** I think my intellectual and emotional sophistication increased considerably. I learned a lot about how businesses go bad and this helped me later when I was working with a charity that ended up going into insolvency. And I learned a lot about relationships, about the dangers of mixing business and pleasure, and about the concept of friendship and what it meant to me. Unfortunately, I think it is highly unlikely I will ever be able to apply this learning to that particular relationship.

4. **Why I am not a failure.** I think I have robustness – it might take me a while to bounce back, but I do. I have good social skills and these have helped me to cultivate other good friends – a success in itself – and because of this, not all my eggs were, at the time my consultancy 'failed', in one basket. My business learning, applied to an insolvent charity, saved a lot of jobs and preserved much of the delivery of service during the rough times we went through. I regard the impact one has as really important and I had more visible, human impact during this time at the charity than in my little consultancy when it went under.

5. **My recommendation.** Be really clear about what is at stake when you go into business with a friend, and take the relevant precautions to make sure you protect yourself and your relationship by working out things in detail beforehand and dealing with them as they arise. Sometimes win-win means the end of the relationship early and not when things are too sour to retrieve. I could establish another consultancy but I doubt I'll ever have that friend back again.

It is an uncertain world, and we never know all the information. So is it such a great surprise that failure is such a common experience? **William Shaw** *tells us about one of his most significant business ventures – and failures.*

1. **My experience of failure.** I launched a magazine in the 1980s without sufficient funding or understanding of where my publisher was sourcing their funding from. For me the biggest part of the failure was that I had employed two people who very quickly became jobless.

2. **How I responded to this failure.** On one level I plunged back into work in order to put it behind me. On the other, I felt very wretched about the whole thing for a long time and it made me, for a while, quite negative about my own ambitions.

3. **What I learned from this failure.** On the downside, it created an aversion to ever being responsible for employing other people. Though I remained friends with both my employees I felt guilty about dragging them in. That has stayed with me and I think I have to count it as a negative. On the positive, it probably left me a little more able to practically assess Greeks who come bearing gifts. It also taught me that what appears to be a catastrophe in June is quickly forgotten by December.

4. Why I am not a failure. I think obviously the foolhardy enthusiasm, which was the weak point in this failure, is a crucial part of success too. I continue to be a big fan of foolhardy optimism.

5. My recommendation. Don't be afraid of asking to look at the books. I was shy about talking about the cashflow of the organisation that employed me and though I had done the maths about the money, my employer clearly hadn't. I am appallingly 'English' about money and it is not a good thing.

Sometimes we do throw the baby out with the bathwater, abandoning something that could have brought us great rewards. **Susan Jones's** *story shows us that a change of perspective can help us understand failure in a new way.*

1. My experience of failure. I failed to continue my practice as an artist in 2002. This was something I had always managed to retain and maintain quality in – regardless of personal and professional interventions – since I had graduated.

2. How I responded to this failure. I struggled to accept my new 'non-practitioner role; I couldn't call myself anything else as a professional, and I denied my 'job title'.

3. What I learned from this failure. I learned that I could apply the same creativity and freedom to 'risk' (which I had experienced in my practice as an artist) to my professional job – and that it actually worked out better when I did. This helped me to understand how imagination and ideas are core business attributes.

4. Why I am not a failure. Because artists have to be self-determining and have to find strategies to deal with failure as a matter of course – the picture didn't work, you've got to sort it out – you can't stop experimenting until it does and the pictures may never work again. Artists have to place themselves at a point of uncertainty as a matter of course, so that the potential for failure is always there. Failure rates are high in the making of art works – in my case maybe one out of six works would fail or everything I did over a particular period of time.

5. My recommendation. It sounds banal but I recommend lateral thinking, critical thinking, walking round and round something to see how it looks from a different perspective.

© Mitch Sava and Jonathan Jewell

CHAPTER 2:
CONCEPTS OF FAILURE
David Hillson

INTRODUCTION

Failure is a big topic. The word has many layers of meaning, and evokes a range of responses from different individuals and groups, depending on their background, circumstances, ambitions, hopes and fears. Some of these varying perspectives are explored in the following chapters, where experts and practitioners from various professions and industries discuss, through illustrative case studies and examples, the specific nature of failure in their area of expertise. Before we get to specifics, however, it is important to cover some introductory common ground, laying out the scope and boundaries of the topic. This should provide a conceptual framework for what follows, putting specific application areas into a wider context, and showing how the various elements of failure relate to one another.

In order to tackle this large concept, this chapter defines failure first in relation to its opposite, success. We then go on to explore some of the key characteristics of failure which might be expected to apply wherever it is encountered. As failure is not a unitary concept, some of the multiple dimensions are then outlined before suggesting some broad ways in which we might tackle failure whenever we come across it.

FAILURE AND SUCCESS

At first sight failure and success are simple opposites. To fail is not to succeed, and success is the absence of failure. But closer examination reveals a complex relationship between these two concepts and that they are not mere antonyms. Understanding how they relate together offers important insights into the nature of failure and how it should be approached. There are two important relationships to consider between failure and success. Firstly, failure starts where success ends and it defines the limits of success. But secondly, success often follows failure, since it frequently occurs after other options have been tried and failed. These two key relationships are described below.

Failure defines limits of success

The first thing to note about failure is that it occurs at the point where we stop succeeding. In other words, we know we are no longer succeeding when we hit our first failure. This might be described as the 'Comfort Success Zone' (CSZ), which can occur in any area of activity or enterprise if we keep succeeding until we fail. This describes the situation where persistent success is bound to lead to failure. If we continue to explore the limits of our CSZ then at some point we will reach a boundary where further success is not possible, as illustrated in Figure 2-1.

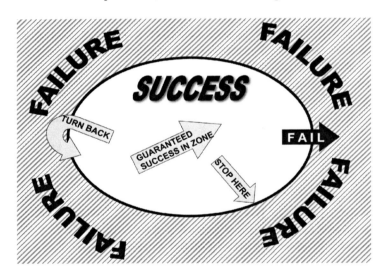

Figure 2-1: The Comfort Success Zone

When we are in a CSZ the optimal behaviour is to investigate the success zone as far as possible, to leave no opportunity unmanaged and no benefit unexploited, until we reach a failure point. The goal is to push our success to the point of failure, and not failing indicates that we are not trying hard enough. As the author T. S. Eliot said, 'Only those who will risk going too far can possibly find out how far one can go.' Science fiction writer Sir Arthur C. Clarke remarked, 'The only way of finding the limits of the possible is by going beyond them into the impossible.' In similar vein, the winning approach of famous Formula One racing driver Mario Andretti was embodied in his view that 'If things seem under control, you're just not going fast enough!' If we always play it safe and remain in our CSZ, then we may not experience failure, but we may also be missing out on possible areas of success that could be easily exploited.

This raises the question of what we should do if we are exploring our CSZ to the point of failure and we come to a boundary. There are of course two options. We could turn back and remain in our CSZ, where we can be confident of further continued success. Or perhaps we should accept the failure and push through it. Maybe something lies beyond the failure zone that marks the edge of the CSZ. This leads us to the second relationship between failure and success.

Success follows limits of failure

The second key insight in the relationship between failure and success is that when one stops failing then one succeeds (unless one stops altogether). This indicates another zone where failure is frequent, but which is finite and which can be traversed into a place of success. Emerging from this Failure Zone (FZ) into success brings us into a new zone where we can discover things that were previously hidden or unavailable.

Here we move beyond the failure that is experienced by others and we begin to learn new ways of succeeding and performing. This might be called the 'Innovation Success Zone' (ISZ). It can be reached by pushing through failure, being prepared to keep on failing until you eventually succeed, as illustrated in Figure 2-2.

Thomas Edison allegedly claimed to have successfully found a hundred ways not to invent the light bulb before ultimately discovering the incandescent filament, indicating the width of the FZ in this specific case before he emerged into the ISZ. While Edison may not have spoken these precise words, the sentiment was echoed by Danish physicist Niels Bohr who defined an expert as 'a person who has made all the mistakes that can be made in a very narrow field' – in other words, someone who has explored the full extent of a particular FZ. More generally, and recognising the need to be prepared to press through the FZ in order to reach the ISZ that lies beyond, Robert Kennedy declared that 'Only those who dare to fail greatly can ever achieve greatly'.

In order to reach the ISZ it is necessary to push through the FZ until success is found. Not succeeding is a result of giving up too soon, losing momentum or running out of energy. Persistence in the face of failure is rewarded eventually with success. As the British wartime Prime Minister Winston Churchill advised, 'If you're going through hell, keep going.'

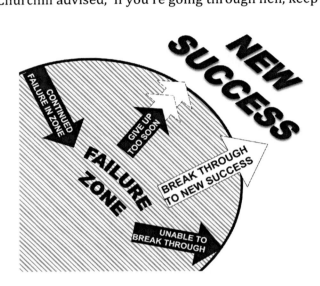

Figure 2-2: The Innovation Success Zone

Of course this is not always the case, and sometimes the FZ is infinitely thick, with no possibility of success beyond it. Or perhaps it is just impenetrable in one direction and a change of tack might lead to breakthrough. The inability to exit the FZ may be due to infeasible goals where success is just not possible or, perhaps, the result of a lack of capability or competence to make the necessary progress through the FZ into success. The famous American comedian W. C. Fields advised 'If at first you don't succeed, try, try again. Then quit. There's no point being a damn fool about it!' The trick is to know when to give up or change direction, and to understand the difference between a situation needing persistence and a pointless quest for unachievable success. This is well expressed in the anonymous Serenity Prayer:

> *God, grant me the serenity to accept the things I cannot change;*
> *The courage to change the things that I can;*
> *And the wisdom to know the difference.*

The Failure Formulae

In simplistic terms, the boundaries between failure and success discussed above can be expressed in two complementary linear formulae (where F represents Failure and S is Success):

$F = S + 1$ (step too far)   (Formula 1)

$S = F + 1$ (extra attempt to succeed)   (Formula 2)

Failure occurs in the Comfort Success Zone (CSZ) when one attempts to do something that is one step too far, taking you beyond the guaranteed success that is found in the CSZ (Formula 1). By contrast, success can be found in the Innovation Success Zone (ISZ) by trying one more time than the number of failures (Formula 2).

These two simple formulae appear to be contradictory and paradoxical. They cannot both be true together unless there is a more complex relationship between failure and success than simply that one is the inverse or absence of the other. Perhaps more complex formulations might reveal additional insights into the relationship between failure and success. For example:

$F = (n \times A_S) + (1 \times A_F)$ (Formula 3)

$S = (n \times A_F) + (1 \times A_S)$ (Formula 4)

In these two formulae, A_S means 'successful attempts', and A_F means 'failed attempts'. 'n' represents the number of those attempts. Formula 3 expands Formula 1, and describes the CSZ, where failure occurs if the number of trials is one failed attempt after the number of successful attempts. Similarly, Formula 4 mirrors Formula 2, with success coming if one tries one more time after all the failed attempts have occurred. The number of attempts can take any value from zero to infinity.

- In Formula 3, if n equals zero then failure is assured – even in the CSZ you cannot succeed without trying. But if n reaches infinity in Formula 3 then failure is impossible, which seems unlikely except in the most exceptional circumstances. Alternatively it may be that the goals are insufficiently challenging and one is simply trying to achieve something trivial or over-easy, and never straying close to the boundaries of the CSZ.

- In the case of Formula 4, n = 0 represents instant success. This describes success on a plate achieved at the first attempt – a rare but conceivable situation. It also reflects a transition from CSZ to ISZ with no additional effort since there is no intervening FZ. By contrast, when n = ∞ then success is impossible – no matter how many times one tries one always fails. This occurs when the goal is unachievable and defeat is inevitable, with an infinite or impenetrable FZ making the ISZ unobtainable.

BALANCING FAILURE AND SUCCESS

We have seen that in the Comfort Success Zone (CSZ), persistent success usually leads to failure. By contrast, in the Innovation Success Zone (ISZ) persistent failure usually leads to success. This describes a mutually synergistic relationship between failure and success where each leads to the other, supporting its opposite. In many ways this complex relationship between failure and success is a typical expression of the Chinese concept of balance, expressed most commonly in yin yang. This suggests that seemingly unconnected or opposing forces are interconnected and interdependent in the natural world, giving rise to each other in turn.

Yin and yang are complementary opposites within a greater whole (expressed in the construction of the Taijitu symbol in Figure 2-3). Everything has both yin and yang aspects, although one element may manifest more strongly in particular objects or at different times. Yin and yang constantly interact, never existing in absolute stasis. Yin yang is used to describe many natural dualities, including dark and light, female and male, low and high, cold and hot. Through the changing proportions of black and white, the Taijitu symbol shows that as one aspect grows stronger the other diminishes. However, the symbol also suggests that when one side is at its strongest it contains an element of the other, indicated by the contrasting dot present at the maximum of its opposite.

Figure 2-3: Taijitu symbol of yin yang

The relationship between failure and success discussed above shows clear yin yang properties, suggesting that instead of being seen as a duality perhaps they should be viewed as two sides of a single unitary phenomenon, and that we would do well to keep both aspects in view and maintain a balanced perspective. If white in the Taijitu symbol represents success and black is failure, then we see success gradually increasing to a point where it leads to failure (characterised above as the threshold between the CSZ and FZ). However we also see that failure increases until it leads to success (emerging from the FZ into the ISZ). It is also, however, usually true that when success flourishes most strongly it contains the seeds of failure, and when we are at the deepest and darkest point of failure then a glimmer of success may be detected.

THE SUCCESS-FAILURE ECOCYCLE

The interrelated yin yang aspects of failure and success can be combined with the concepts of the CSZ and ISZ (described above) to create an oscillating mode, known as the Success-Failure Ecocycle, which switches between failure and success, see Figure 2-4. (The term 'ecocycle' draws on the concept of iterative learning cycles of development from nature. It has been used in recent management literature to describe the need for repeated cycles of performance and learning.)

Here we see that fully exploring the CSZ leads one into the first Failure Zone (FZ): failure defines the limits of success. However, pushing through the first FZ can lead to a new area of success, the ISZ: success follows the limits of failure. The right response on reaching the first ISZ is then to take advantage of the innovation possibilities which it offers, exploiting our new competences and opportunities and consolidating the new insights and benefits. When we spend time in the ISZ, we become familiar and comfortable with it and it becomes our new CSZ within which we can then explore.

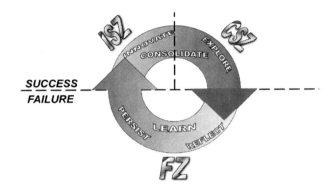

Figure 2-4: The Success-Failure Ecocycle

At this point we can create a repeating cycle, exploring our current CSZ until we reach a FZ, pushing through the FZ into an ISZ, then transforming that ISZ into a new CSZ which we can exploit until we hit a further FZ. This is the expanded Success-Failure Ecocycle shown in Figure 2-5, which is formed from repeated periods of exploration, consolidation and innovation, punctuated by times of failure.

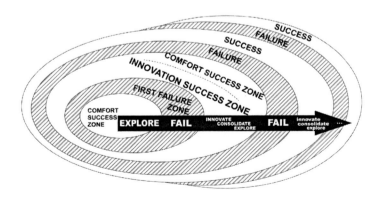

Figure 2-5: The expanded Success-Failure Ecocycle

It is important to recognise this complex relationship between failure and success, rather than simply regarding them as opposites or antonyms. The fact that we should expect continued success to lead eventually to failure will shape our behaviour, as will the understanding that in many (most?) cases we should be able to push through failure to find new success. This concept will become apparent in the chapters that follow, where specific aspects of failure are examined and we learn how they can be handled in a way that brings a degree of success.

TEN CHARACTERISTICS OF FAILURE

The development of the expanded Success-Failure Ecocycle reflecting the yin yang nature of the topic leads to one important conclusion. It is a mistake to think of failure as 'A Bad Thing'. It has a range of negative aspects alongside several positive attributes. These can be summarised into the following ten key characteristics of failure:

1. **Failure is natural.** Failure is an intrinsic part of life, as illustrated by the natural laws of competition and survival of the fittest.

2. **Failure is universal.** Failure can be found everywhere, affecting all facets of human existence, including both personal and corporate activities, in both private and business arenas.

3. **Failure is inevitable.** Perfection is an illusion, a 100% success rate is unattainable, and there will always be more failures than successes.

4. **Failure is pain.** Failure nearly always has negative consequences, and is usually unpleasant for those who experience it.

5. **Failure is opportunity.** Failure offers the chance to draw a line under the past and make a fresh start, stepping out into the future.

6. **Failure is learning.** Failure teaches us where further effort would be wasted, and encourages us not to repeat the same mistakes in the future.

7. **Failure is information.** Failure is a definite result, a clear outcome, indicating what not to do.

8. **Failure is directional.** Failure closes off some potential paths of action, and leaves others open or untried, encouraging us to try something different.

9. **Failure is stimulation.** Failure encourages the human competitive spirit to beat the odds and bounce back with renewed effort, and challenges us to step outside of our comfort zones and experiment, be creative, innovate.

10. **Failure is fun.** Accepting the possibility and likelihood of failure gives freedom to think outside the box, act unconventionally, challenge norms and stereotypes, and be different – which can be very enjoyable!

Of course not all of these characteristics are evident in every instance of failure, or they may appear at different times in the same failure. But these ten statements indicate that it is wrong to think of failure only in negative terms. There are many positive things to take from failure, including its ability to teach us lessons and stop us going in the wrong direction. Indeed the list of ten characteristics above contains more positive statements than negative, suggesting that we might have the balance wrong in the way we think about failure.

This is not to deny the negative, as there is no doubt that failure is usually not welcome, and in some cases it is downright painful – we would all prefer to succeed rather than fail. But most of the negative aspects arise more from the fear of failure than from any particular failure itself. Fear of failure can lead to an over-protective stance, preventing us from taking necessary risks or pursuing profitable opportunities 'just in case it all goes horribly wrong'. This insight leads us to an important characteristic of failure – how you respond to failure is more important than whether you fail or succeed. We will return to this before the end of this chapter.

A TYPOLOGY OF FAILURE

Having explored the complex and synergistic relationship between failure and success and outlined some of the key characteristics of failure, we can now start to consider what types of failure might exist. Initially it is tempting to try to divide failures into two main types: absolute and relative.

- *Absolute failure* is binary: one either succeeds or not, something is right or wrong, pass/fail.

- *Relative failure* describes performance that lies below some threshold: one fails to reach the desired or required standard, or fails in some important aspect or element.

This twofold division appears to be over-simplistic, however, since there are a range of possible dimensions of failure, each of which describes a different element. A particular instance might be a failure in one or more of these dimensions but a success in others. This raises the interesting question of whether a failure in one dimension means an absolute failure, or whether some dimensions are more important than others, or whether there is some negotiable balance to be struck and failure is in the eye of the beholder. Six possible dimensions of failure can be distinguished as follows:

1. **Technical failure** (*'It doesn't work'*). This describes failure to reach a required performance standard, either absolutely ('The engine won't start') or relatively ('It doesn't go fast enough').

2. **Competence failure** (*'I couldn't do it'*). This is a personal failure to achieve some desired or required goal due to lack of ability in some respect.

3. **Moral failure** (*'I cheated'*). It is possible to achieve success in a way that breaks moral or ethical standards, either personally held or societal. Moral failure can occur at individual, group or organisational levels, and might be perceived either absolutely (right and wrong) or relatively (not good enough).

4. **Parameter failure** (*'OK except late/over-budget/too slow...'*). Where there are multiple success criteria it is possible to succeed in some respects and fail in others. In some cases failure against one parameter represents overall failure, and in others it may merely be seen as an acceptable limitation or shortfall.

5. **Hierarchical failure** (*'OK for you but not for me'*). This represents the possibility that something may be perceived as a failure at one level but not at another. Hierarchical failure occurs most often in business or organisations, for example where a project is delivered on time and to budget with the full specification (a project success), but it does not deliver the expected value to the organisation (a business failure).

6. **Subjective failure** (*'I don't like it'*). Sometimes things fail for non-rational reasons, where acceptance criteria of success are subjective or intuitive or hidden or not articulated. In these cases it is possible to meet all success criteria and still be seen as a failure, although the precise reasons may not be clear.

The chapters in Part 2 of this book explore failure in different settings, and examples of each of these dimensions will be evident.

RESPONDING TO FAILURE

Although we can derive some comfort from the fact that failure is not always 'A Bad Thing' – it is not always absolute, and it has many positive characteristics – we might still want to consider how we can respond appropriately to failure. This is a major topic and can be addressed on many levels – indeed it might be a suitable topic for a subsequent book. It is, however, possible to outline one overarching strategy that can be adopted, together with three implementation strands.

The central strategy for dealing appropriately with failure is **resilience**, which needs to be present at individual, group, organisation and societal levels – wherever failure is experienced. The three proposed specific ways to implement resilience can be alliterated as the Three Ms:

- Mindset
- Minimisation
- Maximisation

Resilience

Resilience can be defined as the ability to recover quickly and completely to an original state following a perturbation. More colloquially it might be described as 'The KOKO Factor', since resilience simply requires us to 'Keep On Keeping On'. It can be exhibited by individuals, groups and organisations of various sorts, and at societal level:

- *Individual resilience* has a number of synonyms, including determination, persistence, courage, grit, stickability and bounce-back-ability. It is essentially a blend of inherent personal character, practised emotional literacy and the exercise of will that enables a person to pick themselves up and carry on following unwelcome or difficult circumstances. Resilient individuals are able to take in their stride what life throws at them and carry on towards their goal, although, perhaps, carrying a limp as they bear the consequences of adversity.

- *Group and organisational resilience* is an aspect of shared corporate culture combined with robust processes and grounded values that allows the group to absorb the impact of unforeseen changes or external shocks. It is most evident in the corporate approach to business continuity or disaster recovery, which is targeted, tailored and tried in resilient organisations.

- *Societal resilience* is demonstrated by cultures and societies with a strong sense of identity and shared values as well as internal coherence among and between members of that society across its various strata. When faced with external challenges to its identity or values a resilient society is able to assert those elements that lie at its fundamental core, allowing it to stand firm in the face of threats and maintain its essential existence.

These three layers are hierarchical and nested, with complex interactions and interdependencies, since society consists of various groups, organisations and individuals, and each group or organisation contains other groups as well as individuals. If we could improve our understanding of how these levels of resilience relate together and interact, it would help us to develop enhanced resilience wherever it is needed, for individuals, groups and society.

Much has been written elsewhere about the need for resilience and how to develop it, and it is not necessary to repeat it here. (A helpful starter can be found at www.TestYourRQ.com which introduces the idea of a Resilience Quotient based on research carried out by Jane Clarke and John Nicholson.) Specific examples of the application of resilience in the face of different types of failure are evident in the chapters in Part 2 of this book, as various authors describe how the challenges of failure can be tackled and overcome. Those who survive the challenges of failure are not necessarily the strongest, cleverest, most talented or gifted individuals or groups. Instead they are the ones who know that '90% of success is turning up', and they are prepared to keep going.

There are however three generic implementation themes that can be identified as useful options for developing and deploying resilience in the face of failure. These are briefly outlined below using the Three Ms:

- adopting an appropriate **mindset towards failure**
- taking proactive steps to **minimise the occurrence of failure**
- being sure to **maximise the value obtained** from those failures that do occur

Mindset towards failure

We've seen that failure is inevitable and natural, and it should be expected in any human enterprise that is worth undertaking. We've also seen that failure has a synergistic relationship with success, and the two are inextricably linked. Finally, we've learned that failure has many positive characteristics. Consequently our response to failure should be to expect and accept it. If and when we fail, it is entirely normal and acceptable.

It is more important for us to know how to act in the presence of failure. Here we need to know whether to persist or not. When we encounter a Failure Zone, should we press through looking for the next success, or are we trying to do something unachievable? Knowing when to quit is a key element of an appropriate response to failure. Unfortunately this is not usually a black-and-white matter, and will often involve a subjective judgement. However, the positive aspects of failure might encourage us to persist beyond the first failure, at least to some extent. 'Realistic optimism' is a useful element of the appropriate mindset towards failure, and where this does not come naturally it is possible to develop a response of 'learned optimism' that is more well-founded than mere wishful thinking.

Minimise occurrence of failure

While failure has many upsides, it is not usually our goal to fail. Instead we are seeking success and achievement, and failure blocks our path. Since our goal is to reach the next success zone as quickly as possible, we need to minimise the Failure Zone (FZ) and spend as little time there as possible. We should therefore be seeking strategies to reduce the occurrence of failure as far as is practicable. This is the realm of traditional risk management, and there are many proven approaches, tools and techniques to assist in identifying, understanding, assessing and managing risk.

Much has been written about risk management, but the key points bear repeating here. Risk can be defined as 'uncertainty that matters', and risk management offers a forward-looking radar, scanning the way ahead to identify any future uncertainties that might affect progress towards our objectives. This covers negative uncertainties (threats) that might cause problems if left untreated. But the concept of risk also includes the upside: positive uncertainties (opportunities) that might offer additional value or benefit if we could capture and exploit them. The goal of risk management is to minimise threats, maximise opportunities and optimise the chance of success. Clearly this would result in thinning the FZ and making our path across it as quick and as painless as possible.

Maximise value of failure
The third strategy in responding to failure is to use it to gain as much advantage and information as possible. Failure offers a range of lessons, as indicated by many of the ten characteristics outlined above. It is important for us to take time to capture these valuable lessons and ensure that we learn from our failures. In this way we can build up a body of evidence-based wisdom and experience that we can use to inform our future decisions and behaviour.

In order to implement this strategy we need to build learning time into our routine. Whenever a situation leads to failure, either individually or corporately, we should stop to reflect. What happened here and why? What could/should I/we have done differently? What were the internal and external influences, and can we affect these in future? Who could help me next time I face a similar situation?

Lessons need to be identified, captured and recorded in a way that helps us to remember them in future, so that we can truly become learning individuals and organisations. We need to take the maximum value possible from every instance of failure, turning it into a genuine learning experience, and then we must make any necessary changes to avoid future similar failures.

FINAL THOUGHTS

The Australian actor Paul Hogan is famous for creating the character Crocodile Dundee, with his down-to-earth no nonsense approach to life. In his films the hero faces a wide range of diverse challenges and overcomes them with a winning combination of ingenuity, grit and good humour. In real life Paul Hogan has also faced his challenges, many of which he has overcome in true Dundee-style. He characterises his approach as follows: 'The secret of my success is that I bit off more than I could chew, and chewed as fast as I could!'

This epitomises the approach to failure and success that is recommended in this book. As poet Alfred Lord Tennyson said in his poem *In Memoriam* (1850), ''Tis better to have loved and lost than never to have loved at all.' Or we might quote the well-known motto of the British Special Air Service (SAS) 'Who dares wins.' Or perhaps the words of Churchill might resonate: 'Success is the ability to go from one failure to another with no loss of enthusiasm.'

There seems to be only one sure way to avoid failure and that is never to do anything. But this in itself is failure of a different kind. In this chapter our exploration of the nature of failure and its relationship with success suggests that true failure consists of not trying at all, giving up too soon, or not learning and changing when confronted with failure. Success comes from accepting the reality of failure, taking realistic steps to minimise its occurrence, and learning as much as possible when it does happen. Only when we know how to fail successfully can we become successful failures.

The subsequent chapters in Part 2 provide a rich demonstration of the concepts described in this chapter. Drawing on the insights and experiences of successful failures in a wide range of settings, we learn about failure at individual, group, corporate and societal levels. These chapters show the concept of failure in action and point the way to ensuring that wherever failure is encountered it is addressed successfully.

© David Hillson

PART 2

CHAPTER 3:
PERSONAL FAILURE FROM A
PSYCHOLOGICAL PERSPECTIVE

Marilyn Fryer

INTRODUCTION

Few people like to fail, yet ironically without some failure we would achieve very little in life. Indeed the capacity to fail and to overcome failure is closely bound up with what is perhaps our most important survival technique – our flexibility. It is this capacity which enables us to survive in and adapt to a complex and constantly changing world. This is one of our greatest strengths, but along with our ability to try out alternative solutions and approaches to challenging situations comes the inevitability of failure. Furthermore, without the capacity to fail we would have no free will and would be little more than robots who could only respond in a restricted number of stereotypical ways.

This chapter explores from a psychological perspective:

- Both negative and positive kinds of personal failure and their causes
- Judging failure
- Coping with failure

SOME KINDS AND CAUSES OF PERSONAL FAILURE

There are many different kinds of personal failure. For example, we may be guilty of an unwitting failure, not realising that we have made any mistake at all, unless other people alert us to this or unless some consequence causes us to realise that we have made a mistake. Another example is failure by omission, which may take various forms such as simply forgetting to do something (and this may or may not have repercussions which can range from the trivial to the critical). Alternatively failure by omission may comprise a failure to recognise or capitalise on opportunities or to make the best of one's talents.

Failure as a result of non-response may be because of a feeling of powerlessness in the face of some kind of threat. However, if faced with a severe threat, then failure to act may be the most prudent response – at least initially. In less serious circumstances, the failure to assert one's wishes or rights may simply result from a lack of assertiveness skills. The situations in which people feel able to be assertive vary according to how strongly they feel about an issue, whether they have others' support (if they feel they need it) and the extent to which they think they will succeed. In other words, how much an individual is prepared to risk in any given situation is contingent upon a whole range of factors, some of which may well be outside his or her immediate control.

Failure in its many forms can also be a useful indicator that external help is needed. For example, failure to stop excessively cleaning, tidying or checking doors are locked is often symptomatic of anxiety and, whilst most of us may well exhibit some neurotic symptoms at one time or other, in its severe form an anxiety disorder can be really distressing to the individual concerned who may well feel that his or her life is out of control. Fortunately, with the right help, most anxiety disorders are easily cured. Of more concern is the failure to take any account at all of the effect of one's behaviour on others. In its extreme form (demonstrated by a complete lack of conscience) this can be indicative of psychopathology – something which is far more challenging for the caring professions. Sometimes people deliberately set themselves up to fail, as in the case of 'insecure offenders' such as those described by Fyvel (1961) who often exhibit very low self esteem and who may well do so in order to find the security they seek in a controlled environment such as a prison. At the other extreme, people with a greater than average tolerance of risk are more likely to seek out potentially dangerous activities or indulge in risky business deals.

Ironically, the only sure thing in life is that we will die; everything else embodies a degree of uncertainty about it and hence an element of risk with the attendant possibility of failure. However, it is not psychologically healthy to try to avoid all risks since an excessive fear of risk may be regarded as the most serious of all personal failures. It is, in effect, a failure to embrace life.

Just as there are many different kinds of failure, so there are many different causes. Examples include a lack of training, inadequate attention to detailed instructions or ignorance about what is required. Such ignorance may not be the fault of the individual concerned; it could simply be that other people have not provided him or her with the correct information. Conversely information overload can result in mistakes and accidents as a result of failing to pay special attention to critical information. This latter skill is particularly difficult for people with autism who tend to struggle with filtering out what is irrelevant in the vast amount of data that constantly bombards our senses. They can find it hard to organise such data and experience sensory over-sensitivity to noise or visual stimuli (for instance Grandin, 2006).

However, most of us can make a reasonable job of selectively attending to key information most of the time. When we fail to do so, this can be for a variety of reasons such as boredom, depression or burnout. Distractions can also play a role in this and can cause accidents to occur. People vary in terms of what they find distracting and how distractible they are. At the same time, we are all capable of learning from our mistakes and building up a repertoire of alternative responses. So, although some failure may be inevitable, much is avoidable.

But people do not live and work in a vacuum; context has a role to play and this can range from highly favourable to positively harmful. Indeed in their classic study, Wedge and Prosser (1973) found that some children's environmental circumstances were so adverse (in terms of bad housing, size of family and low income) that they identified them as 'born to fail'. From their research Khokhar & Kumar Upadhayay (2007) concluded that a physically deprived and unhealthy environment can severely disadvantage children and can affect their psychological as well as their physical well being. At the same time it is important to distinguish between economic poverty and physical or psychological deprivation. For example, a home may be economically poor but rich in stimulation for learning and in affection. A very tidy economically rich environment may offer children very little scope for their cognitive development. How this affects their emotional development will depend on the individual circumstances.

The kinds and causes of failure highlighted above serve to illustrate that there are many different causes and consequences of failure which can range from the mildly annoying to the catastrophic. It is also really important to consider the meaning that failure has for the individuals concerned. If they are responsible for a mistake – what was their intention? If they are affected by their own or others' mistakes, how resilient are they and what coping strategies or support networks do they have at their disposal? Only when we appreciate the variables involved in any particular failure scenario can we decide what, if any, action needs to be taken and by whom. Of course not all failure has negative consequences; taking calculated risks and making mistakes enables people to grow.

Although failure isn't necessarily glorious, it can be a precursor of great achievements, acting as a stimulus like the grit in an oyster shell. Indeed Hudson (1966) has argued that it is such grit that stimulates creativity. Successful entrepreneur and social innovator Sir Ernest Hall, who received the RSA's Albert Medal in 1994, has described parts of his early life as characterised by failure or at least by being made to feel a failure (Hall, 2008). In conversation, he also described how on one occasion he had sat round a table with fellow millionaires and observed that before succeeding in their chosen careers they had all failed in some way.

Failure inherent in learning

Indeed failure shouldn't always be regarded as negative, since it is inherent in learning. A common psychological definition of learning is a change in behaviour as a result of experience. When we learn, we have to venture out of our comfort zone into unknown or less familiar territory and this increases the likelihood of failure. But we can learn a great deal from our mistakes as long as they are not so severe as to be inhibiting or, in the worst case scenario, life threatening. To examine the role played by failure in learning, it is useful to consider the different ways in which we learn. They include:

- Trial and error learning and hypothesis testing
- Discovery learning
- Learning as a result of behaviour modification
- Learning through the imitation of 'models'.

Trial and error learning involves what it says – seeing what works and what doesn't and this helps us to build up a mental map of our world. Trial and error learning inevitably involves a great deal of mistakes but, gradually, feedback from our environment (which in its psychological sense denotes everything around the individual, including other people) serves to increase our success rates. Just as we learn from scientific experiments about what works and what doesn't, so in everyday life it is possible learn from our mistakes and move on – to avoid the same or similar pitfalls in the future. Trial and error can be readily observed in the behaviour of young children.

Learning and motivation are closely linked. If the conditions for motivation are good, then any negative effects of failure will be minimised and the positive ones optimised. Motivation comes from a variety of sources such as the tasks we perform, other people's reactions, and our personal goals and strengths. Motivation may be inherent in the task itself (intrinsic motivation) or derived from factors beyond the task (extrinsic motivation).

Tasks that are motivating tend to offer the learner just enough variety or challenge to ward off boredom, but not so much as to be frustrating. The amount of curiosity that a task arouses is a key aspect of intrinsic motivation, and discovery learning is powered by curiosity. Again, just watch young children avidly exploring their environment. Feedback also has an important role to play. The performance of a skilled craftsman tends to decline if he or she cannot get adequate feedback – as when working in a cramped environment for example. Pitting one's wits against one's own past performance and playing the role one wants to play in a group learning situation are also important factors which have a bearing on task-induced motivation (for instance Bruner, 1966).

As far as failure is concerned, motivation and hence learning is likely to diminish if the factors highlighted above are lacking unless we have high levels of belief in our self-efficacy, as defined by Bandura (1997). This means that instead of pursuing one's goals in spite of difficulties, we may well give up, or learn less effectively, unless there are other motivational forces operating i.e. unless we are being adequately motivated by factors outside the task itself.

Extrinsic motivation may be derived from others' reactions to our progress. The whole process of learning and motivation is complex and to go into detail on this here would be to digress unduly. But is it worth noting that behaviour that is appropriately reinforced tends to be repeated up to the point when learning is achieved. Behaviour can be reinforced both by reward (provided this is valued by the individual concerned) and by punishment. Punishment can reinforce undesirable behaviour if it embodies something that the individual being punished values. For example, the negative behaviour of a neglected child may be reinforced by punishment if this means that the child is getting the attention he or she craves and which is normally denied. Once a behaviour has been learned, regular reinforcement is not as effective as intermittent and unpredictable reinforcement (as in gambling).

Behaviour modification sounds 'big brother- ish', but we cannot choose not to have it. It is inherent in all human interaction – whether we like it or not, we are all reinforcing or failing to reinforce one anothers' behaviour all the time. At any one time, the person who is doing the reinforcing is the one who holds the most power. There are several sources of power, for example, charisma, position power, resource power and expertise. Because there are different sources of power, the power base can shift frequently between the partners involved in any human interaction, for example when the topic under discussion changes.

Imitation also plays a role in motivation and learning. The 'models' whose behaviours are imitated by the learner tend to be those whom the learner finds it in some way rewarding to imitate. For example, this may be because:

- they see the model being rewarded for their behaviour
- they are themselves rewarded for behaving in that way
- it feels rewarding to behave like the model.

(Bandura & Walters, 1963.)

Learning through imitation is very evident amongst young siblings where typically the younger child imitates the older child's behaviour. Also, most of us have 'competence models' – people whom we admire and whom we want to be like. Being able to do at least some of the things one's competence model can do can be immensely rewarding to the learner (Bruner, 1966).

Whether or not we are aware of it, we are constantly learning (in everyday life as well as in formal learning situations) and a whole range of motivational factors are operating that affect not only how we learn but how we rate success or failure associated with that learning. Some of our learning is productive but some of it can also be maladaptive.

Failure and expertise

There is a paradox relating to expertise as far as failure is concerned. Throughout history there have been examples of an acknowledged body of experts rejecting novel creative ideas, failing to see their potential simply because they are too steeped in their own tradition and unwilling to entertain alternative ideas or points of view. For example, the uses to which electricity might be put were not immediately recognised; rather, it was seen as merely decorative. However, experts have an advantage over novices when solving complex problems. This is because experts are normally better than novices at recognising patterns, seeing analogies and thinking in terms of underlying principles (Weisberg, 1993). For example in DeGroot's much-quoted study of chess masters, it was noticed that their ability to focus on the correct moves was based on their skill in remembering patterns of moves as opposed to single ones (DeGroot, 1966). It has been found that generally people can cope with about seven chunks of information at a time when solving problems (Cohen, Eysenck and LeVoi, 1986) but chess masters can cope with larger chunks of information than novices can.

Weisberg describes how Chi, Feltovich and Glaser (1981) found the same kind of phenomenon in physics. In this case, the novices focused on the surface appearance of the problems, whereas the professors examined the problems in terms of underlying principles before tackling them. And he compares this with a similar study of radiologists by Lesgold *et al* (1988). Here the experts first identified the kind of problem with which they were dealing and then searched for information that would confirm or reject their hypotheses. Weisberg describes their willingness to flexibly entertain alternative hypotheses to achieve a good match with the evidence before them. However, the novices took much longer to establish an initial diagnosis but, having made it, were reluctant to change it. Indeed, they were more inclined to shape the evidence to match their diagnosis, whilst the experts did the reverse. Weisberg concludes that it is deep immersion in a subject area that enables experts to be aware of underlying principles. The educational implications are discussed in Fryer (1996).

It is worth noting that we are all capable of behaving like novices in areas unfamiliar to us – where we are 'functional illiterates' – and this will increase our tendency to fail. And where we have vested interest in a particular perspective, approach or conclusion, we need to guard against inflexibility.

Failure as an indicator of human performance

When studying human behaviour, psychologists often set people tasks that they will find difficult, or even fail at, in order to slow down their thinking processes so that these can be studied more easily and provide fresh insights into how people think. This data can also be used, for example, to improve the effectiveness of an educational programme by revealing when and how people are getting into difficulty with it.

JUDGING FAILURE

Emergent perceptions of failure

Many years ago, some interesting research into children's emergent understanding of intention and consequence was carried out by the famous psychologist Jean Piaget (for instance, Atkinson *et al*, 1993). Piaget gave young children pairs of moral dilemma stories. In each pair, one told a story in which the consequence of someone's unintended mistake was great; the other story involved a deliberate attempt to mislead which resulted in only a mild mishap. For example, in one story a child trying to be helpful accidentally broke a lot of cups. In the other story a child doing something he shouldn't broke one cup. After each pair of stories, the children were asked which perpetrator was the most naughty. Piaget found distinct differences between the responses of young children (under seven years) and older children. The young children tended to focus on the consequence of failure rather than the intention; the worse the outcome, the naughtier it was perceived. In contrast, the older children were more able to take account of both intention and consequence when evaluating the scenarios.

Interestingly, Piaget's findings on children's developing sense of morality is in keeping with his findings with regard to spatial awareness in which he found that older children could cope with two variables at a time (as when sorting blocks in terms of both size and colour) whereas the young children could only focus on one variable at a time.

The older children also had more sophisticated views about punishment. Fairness was very important to them. They wouldn't, for example, accept that punishing a whole class for the wrong-doings of some of the class members was fair. The young children on the other hand believed that adults could do no wrong and the more severe the punishment, the better.

Piaget also describes how, as children mature, they become fascinated by rules and enjoy inventing rules for the games they play. Unlike young children, they no longer regard rules as fixed and predetermined.

Building on Piaget's work, Kohlberg sought to develop a more sophisticated model of young people's progressive sense of morality. Both Piaget's and Kohlberg's work have been criticised for different reasons, but they each shed some light on children's emergent understanding of morality and the way in which mistakes can be viewed.

Who can judge?

In one sense it makes little sense to consider who may legitimately judge people's behaviour in order to assess whether or not they have failed, since people will judge themselves and others anyway and their evaluations will range from the plausible to the implausible. Societal laws rules and norms also have roles to play. Whether or not we accept these as legitimate will depend, at least partially, on how open and tolerant our society is, whether we regard the laws and customs of our society as just and how independent we feel. In this latter regard, Jahoda's classification of dependence/independence is highly relevant to any consideration of the extent to which people are likely to risk failure and hence possible censure (Jahoda, 1959). For example, Jahoda distinguishes between secure and insecure independents.

If we are called upon to formally judge others' performance, as teachers are for example, then it is important, for young people's psychological well-being, to distinguish between our feelings for the individual concerned and their behaviour. Similarly, it is important that parents and carers reassure children that they still love them even when they do not always condone their behaviour (for instance, Rogers & Freiberg, 1994; Rogers, 1983).

As adults, how we react to external criticism is likely to depend, at least in part, on how much we value the critic's opinion of us, as well as how confident we are and what other relevant personality attributes we have.

COPING WITH FAILURE

Figure 3-1: Strategies for coping with failure

The extent to which people have good support systems and a ready repertoire of coping strategies will also have a bearing on both how concerned they are about failure and their willingness to take risks. Similarly the capacity to think creatively (e.g. to envisage alternative routes to a solution) can boost people's confidence to take *calculated risks* (for instance, Sturner, 1990). A good repertoire of problem solving skills is an enormous help since this helps people solve intransigent problems and cope with uncertainty, and these skills can be learned.

Two other factors have a bearing on our ability to cope with failure: our personality characteristics and our learning (cognitive) styles.

Personality may be defined as a 'set of enduring characteristics'. Many different attributes affect how people cope with failure. For example, the more secure and self confident people are, the less likely they are to be concerned about the errors they make. But, although we do have habitual ways of responding, our self confidence can, to an extent, vary with circumstance and it is possible for the same individual to feel really confident in one situation and much less confident in another. Additionally, self esteem (how one feels about oneself) develops very early on. Indeed, early relationships have an important role to play in helping children grow up feeling loved and secure. Ironically, just at the time when young children most fear separation from their parents or main carers (at around sixth months to a year) working mothers often have to return to work. So, to avoid undue separation anxiety, young children need to have developed a strong bond with one or a few alternative carers from a very early age – or else avoidable lengthy separations need to be delayed until the child is older. Otherwise government policies designed to increase the economic prosperity of a household by encouraging both parents to work full-time can have an adverse effect on the self confidence of growing children and their subsequent ability to cope with adversity.

Additionally, we all exhibit a range of cognitive styles (habitual ways of thinking) that can affect both whether we are likely to fail and how we respond to failure. The identification of 'cognitive styles' is one means of categorising human behaviour. Two things are important to note. Firstly, any categorisation involves simplification – in other words it involves ignoring idiosyncratic data and focusing on commonalities. Secondly, psychologists operating from different theoretical perspectives have labelled the same behavioural phenomena in different ways. Additionally, there is some overlap in the categorisation of cognitive styles i.e. different psychologists have cut the same 'pie' of human behaviour in slightly different ways.

One example of a cognitive style is 'category width'. Pettigrew (1958) found that people varied in terms of the range of items they tended to take into account when coming to a decision and he devised a 'category width scale', which is still popular, to assess this. Those who score high on category width (i.e. who are more able to take account of a large number of variables) are better able to cope with failure since this facility helps them to envisage a greater number of connections or alternative solutions. Those who score low on category width have a greater tendency to respond in stereotypical ways. Not surprisingly highly creative people tend to score higher on this measure of cognitive style. However, in a sense, both high and low scorers experience some failure. The high scorers do so because quite a few of the ideas they are willing to entertain are likely to be irrelevant; the low scorers fail because they are only willing to entertain a limited number of ideas, rejecting some which could have been useful.

To take another example, some people are more reflective than others and this tendency to be less impulsive, to think before acting, has been found to develop with age (Kagan, 1966). Closely linked to impulsivity is the capacity to exhibit 'inconsequential behaviour' as discussed in Stott's classic study (Stott, 1966). Inconsequential behaviour involves a failure to consider the consequences of one's actions. So, for example, a young man may jump off a roof without thinking what will happen to him if he does. Or inconsequential behaviour may also be the result of drug-induced distorted perceptions.

Our habitual ways of thinking can be either helpful or counter-productive in enabling us to cope with failure or even to avoid failure altogether. However, if we are failing to make *any* mistakes the chances are we are being too cautious, not stepping out of our comfort zone, or else we are being over-protected by other people.

CONCLUSION

The variables involved in any failure situation include type of failure, intention, causes and consequences, and contextual factors. How these affect the individual or individuals concerned will be contingent on a whole range of factors such as self esteem, self confidence, motivation, the capacity to think creatively, personality factors and cognitive styles. So is there any sense in which failure may be seen as glorious? Arguably yes – when it demonstrates independent thought, a willingness to experiment, to try alternative approaches en route to one that works and to persist in the face of setbacks and adverse criticism. As has been argued, failure and risk are a necessary part of human development. But risk *per se* is not necessarily going to lead to positive outcomes. Calculated risks may do. However, the greatest failure is inaction in the face of opportunity: failure to engage in living and to discover what might be.

References

Atkinson, L., Atkinson, R. C., Smith. E. E., & Benn, D. J. (1993). *Introduction to Psychology Eleventh Edition*. Fort Worth, Texas: Harcourt, Brace, Jovanovich.

Bandura, A. (1997). *Self-efficacy: The Exercise of Control*. New York: W. H. Freeman.

Bandura, A. & Walters, R. (1963). *Social Learning and Personality Development*. New York: Holt, Rinehart & Winston.

Bruner, J. S. (1966). 'The will to learn'. In J. M. Whitehead (1975) *Personality and Learning Volume 1*. London: Hodder & Stoughton & the Open University.

Chi, M., Feltovich, P. J., & Glaser, R. (1981). 'Categorization and representation of physics problems by experts and novices'. *Cognitive Science* (5) 121-5.

Cohen, G. Eysenck, M. W. & LeVoi, M. E. (1986). *Memory: A Cognitive Approach.* Milton Keynes: Open University Press.

DeGroot, A. (1966). 'Perception and memory versus thought: some old ideas and recent findings'. In B. Kleinmuntz (Ed.) *Problem Solving Research, Method and Theory.* New York: Wiley.

Fryer, M. (1996). *Creative Teaching and Learning.* London: PCP at Sage.

Fyvel, T. R. (1961). *The Insecure Offenders: Rebellious Youth in the Welfare State.* London: Chatto & Windus.

Grandin, T. (2006). *Thinking in Pictures, Expanded Edition: My Life with Autism.* Vintage.

Hall, E. (2008). *How to be a Failure and Succeed.* Brighton: Book Guild Publishing.

Hudson, L. (1966). *Contrary Imaginations.* London: Methuen.

Jahoda, M. (1959). 'Conformity and independence: a psychological analysis'. *Human Relations.* (12) 99-120.

Kagan, J. (1966) 'Reflection – impulsivity: the generality and dynamics of conceptual tempo'. *Journal of Abnormal Psychology.* 71 (1) 17-24.

Khokhar, C. P. & Kumar Upadhayay, B. (2007). 'Poor physical environment and the adjustment of adolescents'. *Europe's Journal of Psychology.*

Lesgold, A. et al. (1988). 'Expertise in a complex skill: diagnosing X-ray pictures'. In M. T. H. Chi, R. Glaser and M. Farr (Eds.) *The Nature of Expertise.* Hillsdale, NJ: Erlbaum.

Pettigrew, T. F. (1958). 'The measurement and correlates of category width as a cognitive variable'. *Journal of Personality.* (26) 532-544.

Rogers, C. R. & Freiberg, H. J. (1994). *Freedom to Learn, 3rd Edition.* Columbus OH: Charles Merrill Publishing Co.

Rogers, C. R. (1983). *Freedom to Learn for the 80's.* Columbus OH: Charles Merrill Publishing Co.

Stott, D. H. (1966). *Studies of Troublesome Children.* Taylor & Francis.

Sturner, W. (1990). *Calculated Risk: Strategies for Managing Change.* Buffalo: Bearly.

Wedge, P. & Prosser, H. (1973). *Born to Fail.* Arrow Books in association with the National Children's Bureau.

Weisberg, R. W. (1993). *Creativity: Beyond the Myth of Genius.* New York: Freeman.

CHAPTER 4:
SOCIETAL FAILURE:
IS THERE SUCH A THING?
Cliff Leach

There is no such thing as society: there are individual men and women, and there are families.
Margaret Thatcher, 1987

The central task I have set myself and this party is to be as radical in social reform as Margaret Thatcher was in economic reform. That's how we plan to repair our broken society.
David Cameron, 2008

INTRODUCTION

Most societies are the products of organic and accidental growth and evolution rather than the outcome of some process of design and control; they are the result of the wisdom of the crowd rather than the notions of the elite and are influenced by a host of factors such as economics, religion, politics and even the weather.

So the key question for me is *Can a society be considered to fail?* If there are no predetermined criteria for success, no initial specification against which to define completion and no preset goals to meet, then what does societal failure mean? Furthermore, would 'success' in those terms be a desirable outcome at all? It might be the goal of any utopian world view, but are utopias realistic or desirable?

In researching this area I looked at a wide range of sources and reviewed a lot of literature, not least the host of information on 'failed nation states' and the wealth of commentary on British society, so often described (both now and throughout history) as 'broken'.

Lurking at the back of my mind has been the uncanny notion that the success of a society is much like good taste or good art – we know it when we see it, just as we know when it is not working – but defining this is somewhat more problematic, context dependent and subjective.

Clearly there are some areas capable of examination and comparison when considering societal failure. Though rough and ready the criteria I have chosen are:

- Objectives – what the society seeks to achieve, either by design or innately emerging as a function of some self-organising property.
- Stakeholders – who are involved in the society and more particularly who have something to gain or lose as a result.
- Standards – what social failure looks like and what costs are acceptable for success.

In this chapter I apply these criteria to two example societies that might be viewed as failures. These examples are the USSR (1922-1991) and colonial penal Australia (1780-1880). It is, however, immediately obvious that such a complex area cannot be simply assessed. The criteria for the success of my two primary examples were completely different, as is the evaluation of their degree of failure or success.

EXAMPLE 1: USSR (SOVIET UNION)

A brief summary of the Soviet Union

I'm going to start in recent history with the Soviet Union, a society that was designed from fundamental political ideology but one which was built on the foundations of an older medieval system and which extended beyond the boundaries of its origins in Russia.

The Union of Soviet Socialist Republics (USSR) was a socialist state that formed following a period of bloody revolution and lasted for 69 years from 1922 to 1991. The term 'soviet' refers to a council, the notional foundation for this particular form of socialist society. From this description one might consider it to be an inclusive approach taking into account the needs of all the stakeholders, though the reality was more complex.

Whilst the Soviet Union was constitutionally a Commonwealth of fifteen theoretically autonomous republics, the Russian Soviet Republic's economic, geographic and military dominance meant that the USSR was more specifically 'Russian' than broadly 'Soviet'.

Emerging after World War I and following the collapse of the Old Russian Empire as a consequence of the Russian Revolution and the Russian Civil War, Vladimir Lenin won control of most of the Old Russian Empire. After his death, power moved to Josef Stalin who implemented a command economy and, using brutal methods, forced Soviet society through large-scale industrialisation.

The Soviet Union led an aggressive and expansionist foreign policy but following their attack on Poland, Finland and the Baltic countries in 1939-1940, the Soviet Union itself was attacked in 1941 by Germany (theoretically an ally at the time). After four years of brutal and all-out war the Soviet Union finally emerged as one of the world's two superpowers alongside the USA, having occupied a large section of Eastern Europe and installed or backed Russian-Soviet (and largely 'puppet') governments in these countries.

The post second world war period was marked out both by the 'cold war' – a terrifying ideological, political and overtly military struggle between the USSR and the communist countries on the one side and the United States and the West on the other side. This period was also defined by the last years of Stalin's terrifying regime and its legacy of political and social repressions that led to the atrocities of the gulags and other violent and brutal methods of social central control.

Despite its meteoric early rise, the Soviet Union began to unravel during the 1980s. Mikhail Gorbachev took control of the Soviet Union in 1985 and tried to initiate fundamental reforms in the economic, social and political machinery of the Soviet Union. However, Gorbachev failed in his attempts at unity and change and in 1990-91 the Soviet Union disintegrated. Remembering where one was when the Berlin Wall fell is up there with the assassination of J. F. Kennedy and the moon landing as a seminal moment in life and part of the shared social history of the peoples of the world.

Soviet Union: societal failure or societal success?

So was the Soviet Union a societal success? Well first of all let's look at the objectives of the state.

The state was formed as a direct response (via revolution) to the repressive and reactionary (and largely feudal) situation in Russia. The key objectives of the formation of the Soviet state were the redistribution of wealth, power and decision-making, and the removal of a capital-owning and class-based system of social deference and control. In a nutshell it was intended to make life for the masses of Russian people better, not just for the short term but in perpetuity.

Life and death in the Soviet Union

Some statistics are enlightening here. Life expectancy could be considered as one of the simplest indicators of societal success. Following the revolution life expectancy for all age groups improved.

Birth year	1890-1900	1920-1930	1950-1960
Life expectancy	33 years	44 years	68 years

Of course this does not prove that the Soviet system was any more successful than the general run of other more typically capitalist systems. The trend continued into the 1960s, when the life expectancy in the Soviet Union was marginally longer than the life expectancy in the United States. However, from 1964 the trend seems to have changed and though life expectancy for women remained relatively stable, it declined significantly for men.

The improvement in infant mortality also levelled out and then began to rise. This may be explained by the number of pregnancies in the Asian part of the USSR where infant mortality was highest, while the number of pregnancies was lower in the more developed West of the Soviet Union.

So it would seem, from this perspective alone that the Soviet Union was a reasonable success, albeit one of declining efficacy into the last decade of the 20th Century. For those who lost status, power and wealth (and often their lives) the picture would be negative. However I have found no reliable statistics for post 1990.

Against this apparent improvement of life expectancy must be balanced the actions of this totalitarian state which conducted extensive human rights abuses, and where tens of millions were sent to concentration camps, the gulags and otherwise exterminated. Estimates of the death toll during the Stalin era alone amount to at least 20 million people.

Power and the people in the Soviet Union

Another attribute of societal success is the freedom enjoyed by individuals and their security under the law. The Soviet political and economic systems were dominated by the Marxist-Leninist Soviet Communist Party. This was the Soviet Union's state party, and the only permitted party.

The politics of the Soviet Union started in an earnest attempt at mass enfranchisement. It ended in a corrupt and totalitarian regime ossified and unable to react to a changing world and ignoring the reasonable desires of the population for more diverse political structures and representation.

The Secretary of the party was more powerful than the government or the parliament, and the people of the Soviet Union had very little real political freedom. The secret intelligence services of the KGB and the police as well as organised systems of informants monitored anyone and everyone that came to note. So it seems reasonable to conclude that representation of the people and by the people was not delivered as originally envisaged and can be seen as a failure of the Soviet social system.

Business and employment

Business (in terms that would be understood in the West) in the Soviet era was virtually nonexistent and almost all business was both State owned and run. Typified by poor quality, high costs and outdated production it was more of a joke than a reality in the communist times. Today Russia is driving forward (though the same cannot be said for all of the previous Soviet Union countries), but this is more through extractive industries than productive ones.

Though the Soviet era was a failure for business in the traditional capitalist sense and moreover was so by design, unemployment on the other hand was almost unknown in the Soviet Union, where over-employment was more often the case. So while 'business' may have failed as a societal outcome of the Soviet era, livelihood scored rather better.

While the Soviet Union was at its best a well-developed social system with universal health care provision and social support, it left behind a legacy of fragmented power and social inequality. While some people yearned for the past and the certainties of Stalin's rule, others welcomed the emergence of a new but small and obscenely wealthy capitalist elite. Sadly for the rural poor of Russia and the other former Soviet member states, life seems in many ways to be going backwards not forwards and social inequality appears to be growing.

Final score on the Soviet Union

In summary, the Soviet experience may have been positive for many, and it certainly moved the mass of the populations of the countries involved from feudal medievalism into the 20th Century. However it foundered when the problems of ego and nepotism coupled with the impossibility of running a planned political economy overwhelmed the organs of government and the remains of the system collapsed back into something more akin to *laissez-faire* capitalism.

Business was near nonexistent, but then in the Soviet model business was an anathema and the society it formed did result in a single and more equal model than its predecessor. Weighing this up, on balance it could be viewed as successful, though it was unacceptably costly in human life and suffering. It is of course impossible to know whether any of the alternative routes open in 1917 would have been any better or less painful or even possible in the circumstances.

In reviewing my initial criteria:

Did the USSR meet its objectives? The answer is yes but in part. The removal of a feudal regime with its vast inequalities and the creation of a more representative (though very imperfect) state was achieved. A key objective was the creation of a centrally planned economy and this too was achieved, though only to prove the impossibility of managing and administering such a model. If we leave the massive costs in lives and suffering of the Stalinist era to one side, things were better for the masses at the end of the Soviet era than at the start in many, though not all, areas of life.

Did the USSR satisfy and serve its stakeholders? Here the answer is mixed. It did (as highlighted above) deliver some positive outcomes for many of its citizens, although this was at great economic and human cost. It is impossible to determine if any other method of regime change would have achieved the same outcomes, but with lower costs in lives and misery. I am of the view that the Stalinist era was largely (though not entirely) a function of Stalin himself rather than an inevitable outcome of the political system at the time.

Did the USSR adhere to standards? Certainly the costs of change were very great for those caught up in the changes and in the brutality of revolution and warfare. My gut reaction is that the cost in lives could not justify the outcomes achieved, especially by comparison to other possibilities such as a gradual modernisation of Russia in response to trade and commerce with the wider world. The high-minded philosophy of the early revolution was simply lost in the messy and factionalised implementation of change in Russia and the wider Soviet Union. By its own political standards, the most basic of which stated that those who are able do what they can and those in need get what they need, the Soviet Union largely failed and most certainly could not go on into the 21st Century.

EXAMPLE 2: COLONIAL PENAL AUSTRALIA

Another 'designed' society was that of Australia in the period 1780 until 1880 – the period of British colonisation and of Australian Penal history. This is one of the rare examples of a closely controlled and well documented experiment in social engineering.

The land Cook reported

Australia has been inhabited for over 40,000 years, probably via migration from the Southeast Asian area. At the time of European settlement in the 18th century, most indigenous Australians were hunter-gatherers, with an oral culture and spiritual values based on reverence for the land but lacking any comparable views of ownership or property to those of their European colonisers.

In 1770 James Cook sailed around and mapped the east coast of Australia, which he named New South Wales and claimed for Great Britain. It was Cook's discoveries which whetted the British appetite for colonial expansion and then prepared the way for establishment of a new penal colony.

The British Crown Colony of New South Wales began as a settlement at Port Jackson by Captain Arthur Phillip on 26 January 1788. This date was later to become Australia's national day, Australia Day. Van Diemen's Land, now known as Tasmania, was later settled in 1803 and became a separate colony in 1825. The United Kingdom formally claimed the western territories of Australia in 1829.

Prisons full to bursting

There were clear objectives in the establishment of Australia as a penal colony. At the close of the 18th century Britain had major social problems and unrest with rising levels of detected and prosecuted crime (partly as a result of more professional policing), coupled with crippling war debts and very hard-line attitudes on criminality. This period saw a great increase both in the number of offences carrying a capital sentence and in the numbers of offenders sent to jail or convicted to hang for petty offences (the so-called 'bloody code'). Soon the jails were overflowing with inmates and the gallows were doing a brisk trade in judicial execution.

In a desperate attempt to address the problems of overcrowded jails by a society unable or unwilling to build new ones ('Not In My Back Yard' was an attitude just as prevalent then as now), old warships, denuded of masts and rigging were anchored close to land and employed as makeshift prisons (the infamous 'Hulks'). However these too soon became overcrowded to an unusable degree.

One form of deportation – indentured servitude (effectively licensed slavery of prisoners for a defined period of time to free British settlers in colonial America) – was used to send around 50,000 convicts from the UK until the American war of independence closed off that avenue.

The Australian solution

The key objectives that emerged in the establishment of Australia as a British penal colony were:

- The creation of a cheaper alternative to building jails in the UK and as a replacement for indentured servitude after the American War of Independence 1775-1783.
- An alternative to both jail and capital punishment that was an effective deterrent.
- The settlement of Australia and domestication of its lands and indigenous peoples.
- Preventing the French getting a foothold in the area.
- As an alternative to America for entrepreneurs looking for opportunity.

The main stakeholders in this experiment in social engineering were:

- The Aboriginal peoples of Australia.
- The convicts themselves and their families.
- The people of the UK.
- The free settlers.
- The Navy and Army who had the task of transportation and of running the penal colony.

Deterrent and detention

Certainly the establishment of the colony was initially a cheaper alternative to building and running prisons in the UK, and it was certainly more popular with anyone in the vicinity of a proposed new prison. About 160,000 men and women were brought to Australia as convicts from 1788 until penal transportation finally ended in 1868 (this was somewhat piecemeal across the various areas of Australia from 1848 onwards).

In the early 1790s, the convicts were joined by free immigrants. The wool industry and the gold rushes of the 1850s both provided an impetus for increasing numbers of free settlers to go to Australia.

As for the efficacy of the deterrent effect of the Australian penal colony, it is difficult to assess but there appeared to be little or no positive impact. Crime in the UK continued to rise, including violent *'crimes against the person'*. A surge in the convict population was further exacerbated after the formation of formal policing in Britain in 1829 in London and then by 1857 throughout Britain which in turn led to more effective detection and conviction.

The regime employed in the British penal colony of Australia was brutal in the extreme, and especially so for anyone committing further offences while serving out their sentence of transportation and selected for secondary punishments.

On Norfolk Island, Van Diemen's Land (Tasmania) or one of the mainland secondary punishment establishments, there was a short period where a brief attempt at more humane penal treatment was implemented, but floggings and beatings along with solitary confinement, starvation and exposure became the norm and in many cases, killed the unfortunate miscreants. Hangings were commonplace. This was a dark, savage and shameful period in British history.

Sentences were typically 7 or 14 years and, less frequently, transportation for life. However, prisoners with good behaviour, and especially those with valuable skills or trades, might earn a commutation of their sentences, the much valued 'ticket' or even a complete pardon, following which it was possible to return home to Britain. Interestingly, at the end of their sentence just 7% of those entitled to go back ever did so; a damning indictment of the social conditions left behind as much as the opportunities presented in Australia. The apparent conclusion is that transportation was not much of a deterrent.

Settlement and economic performance

The French never got a foothold in the area, though perhaps because they could see no strategic value in it and had enough problems of their own from 1815 onwards with the end of the Napoleonic war.

The economics of the penal colony were based on prisoners being used as free labour by the free settlers, in return for which the settlers were expected to oversee them and eventually feed and clothe them. This was simply a cheap outsourcing deal on the part of the British and was something that could be withdrawn at any moment and on a whim by the local powers and institutions. Unlike the certainties afforded to the Americans through the indentured servitude labour or slavery systems, where there was certainty of the supply and availability of labour through the horrors of human bondage, the Australian settler could and often did fall foul of powerful and capricious interests which could leave them with land but no labour in an instant. This was a system fraught with risk for any settler, and was both corrupt and nepotistic at times.

With such uncertainties few settlers invested for the long term and with a few notable exceptions the Australian economy initially was a net drain on the British exchequer. This all changed in 1848 when someone found gold. Guards and farmers, school teachers and marines – in fact everyone and anyone – deserted their posts to dig for their fortune and the country suddenly grew rich on the proceeds. With new wealth came a new confidence which began to assert itself and slowly modern Australia started to emerge from the British colonial penal social experiment.

Eventually, through the changing of social attitudes in Britain, the growth of a more mature prison system, the improvements of the British economy and the rapid growth in numbers of free settlers into Australia, the penal-colonial system fell apart and transportation finally ended in 1868.

Impact on the indigenous Australian people

The settlement of Australia domesticated its lands but at terrible and irreversible cost to its indigenous peoples. When Europeans first arrived there were somewhere between 350,000 and 750,000 Aboriginal people. By 1900 their population had declined to around 90,000.

In some areas such as Van Diemen's land these people were almost exterminated through a mixture of disease (particularly smallpox), changes in the natural environment for farming use and outright murder.

Typical of the disdain with which the Aboriginal peoples were treated at that time is the example of Truganini, the last Tasmanian Aborigine, whose skeleton was exhumed within 2 years of her death in 1876 by the Royal Society of Tasmania, and was later placed on display.

Final score on colonial penal Australia

How did this experiment in designing and building a rigidly controlled society all score? At a massive cost in human misery for the convicts, their families and the native Aborigines, it failed to have any impact on crime. The domestication of the land could probably have been achieved in a more humane manner. But for many (93% in fact) of the prisoners who made it through the trials of transportation, it perhaps was no worse than life back home, and for some it was much better and led to a good life and, for a very few, to personal riches and success.

Looking at Australia's penal history and origins, did it achieve its objectives? It clearly did achieve many in that it removed a problem from Britain, was a cheaper option than prison building (financially and politically) and did create a presence in the Southern hemisphere before the French could do so. But these explicit objectives were there to achieve a reduction in crime and disorder in Britain – little accurate statistical criminological evidence is available for the early period (1780-1830) – but anecdotal evidence suggests the crime wave continued.

As for the stakeholders, things were very mixed indeed. For the British establishment, though costs were reduced and political problems shifted (including providing the Crown with a handy popular alternative to judicial execution), eventually, both for the reasons outlined above and due to a shift in public attitudes, the Australian alternative became untenable. The prisoners themselves had a very rough time, yet, as mentioned earlier, their reluctance to accept the option of repatriation in any meaningful number could be construed as an unintended positive outcome for many. For the indigenous Australian aboriginal people, the outcome was catastrophic. Overall then a pretty poor score.

The ethical, social and judicial standards by which the regime of penal Australia was developed were very different from those of today. But those more brutal and less humane/liberal standards were consistent with the wider standards of the time.

However, when we scratch the surface it is clear that even by those standards the sheer brutality, corruption, nepotism and capriciousness of the regime were a failure of management and of meeting the standards that ought to have been applied.

SOCIETY AND FAILURE REVISITED

In thinking about this area one thing becomes clear: were a society to succeed, that is to achieve some set of designed criteria for success, it would then either have to stagnate and essentially become a utopia in aspic, or it would have to fail by eventually being unable to adapt those criteria as they became irrelevant in the face of changing circumstances.

If there is anything that comes out of an investigation into this area, albeit a very brief one, it is that societal success is a capability of a society or a social system, not an outcome of one. If I have to define success for a society it is the ability of the social system to adapt to the needs of changing circumstances but at the most acceptable cost to the people within it.

In these terms, the example of Australia as a colonial penal settlement which led to a vibrant, successful and democratic country shows how from the failure of one society (that of the British penal colonisation as well as the subjugation of the aboriginal people) can develop into a society which by most measures of fairness, economics, and progress can claim to be reasonably, though not perfectly, a success.

The Soviet situation was somewhat different. What remains now from the old Soviet Union are countries with very different levels of success. Russia is moving quickly towards a strong economy that one hopes offers a potential for major improvements in the standards of living for its people. Sadly, some other Former Soviet Union (FSU) countries are far less successful.

Many factors accounted for the demise of both systems, but one thing stands out: the influence of global events and interests. For the Soviet Union it was economics and a grass roots movement towards consumerism and social change. For colonial Australia it was hitting economic take-off speed after striking gold and gaining the confidence to push back against British interests.

So what might this mean for modern Britain? We live in a more globally connected society today than at any other time in human history, and because of this the context within which British society has to operate is becoming more flexible and dynamic and less predictable.

It seems clear to me that a healthy, sustainable and therefore successful British society is one that can adequately and acceptably respond to that context and deliver the best outcomes for the people within it. Here we have the nub of a problem: both Soviet and British colonial examples have one thing in common: they were both centrally planned command-driven societies. Both established their systems quickly and both became the dominant social models in their areas, because of this command-based approach. Both failed for the same key reason; when society starts to grow it cannot be controlled for long and it starts to self-organise.

This is not a radical argument for anarchy however, but it is a recognition that any successful society is one that engages its members and in which they actively participate. More than ever we seem to need social engagement from all in our midst, more now than ever do we all rely on each other to find and implement the solutions to our social problems and to deliver the kind of society that we want for ourselves and our children.

The key theme of British society following the 2010 election seems to be social engagement; a recognition that government can only do so much and that ultimately social cohesion, like social order, is one of consensus. Building this consensus and engaging people requires many things, not the least of which is a change in behaviour and aspiration from many people in our society. This is easy to say but extremely difficult to achieve and though political leaders rightly point to the need for this engagement and the power of mobilising such a force, political action through compulsion (however enacted) is likely to tempt any administration.

Societies, whether Britain today or those in extremis cited above, seem to have a centre of gravity, a focus that shifts slowly and reflects the consensus of behaviour and belief within those societies.

Though the Soviet Union and the Australian penal colonial systems fell in a few decades, most social change takes much longer and can only be seen through historic reflection. This implies that part of our problem is one of patience. If viable long-term change in society can only come from within and if it takes generations to occur, then the political system must recognise the need for planning for this change, as well as providing the drive towards the social standards that underpin it and the investment in actions that only deliver in a future we will not live to see.

However, it was the suicide of one oppressed and unemployed man in Tunisia (Mohamed Bouazizi, who burned himself to death in December 2010) that led to protests resulting initially in the downfall of President Zine al-Abidine Ben Ali and then in an avalanche of protest and discontent throughout the wider region. Even in the most despotic and highly organised of societies, it is the wisdom and will of the crowd that prevails and that, when triggered by some small but iconic event, can achieve rapid social change. Let us all hope that having thrown out the old, the region can create something better in the new.

I disagree with Mrs Thatcher's dictum; there is such a thing as society and it has its part to play in all our lives, but it is we the people that must call the tune and we the people that have to agree and keep to the standards, however inconvenient to our day to day behaviours. I am sure our politicians know this, I'm sure most people know it too, we just all have to be honest and agree about it and start living in the knowledge that we borrow our place on the planet until the next generation comes along.

References

Emsley, C. (1996). *Crime and English Society 1750-1900, 2nd edition.* Longman.

Emsley, C. (1996). *The English Police: A Political and Social History, 2nd edition.* Longman.

Gilbert, M. (2002). *The Routledge Atlas of Russian History.* London: Routledge.

Hughes, R. (1987). *The Fatal Shore.* Alfred A. Knopf Inc.

London, J. (2001). *The People of the Abyss.* Penguin Classics (First published 1903).

Mayhew, H. (1985). *London Labour and the London Poor.* Penguin Classics.

Orlov, D. (2008). *Reinventing Collapse.* New Society Books.

Radzinowicz, L. and Hood, R. (1990). *The Emergence of Penal Policy in Victorian and Edwardian England.* Clarendon Press.

Robb, G. (1992). *White-Collar Crime in Modern England: Financial Fraud and Business Morality 1845-1929.* Cambridge University Press.

Shore, H. (1999). *Artful Dodgers: Youth and Crime in Early Nineteenth-Century London.* Boydell Press/Royal Historical Society.

Sindall, R. (1990). *Street Violence in the Nineteenth Century: Media Panic or Real Danger?* Leicester University Press.

Taylor, D. (1997). *The New Police in Nineteenth-Century England: Crime, conflict and control.* Manchester University Press.

Taylor, D. (1998). *Crime, policing and punishment in England 1750-1914.* Macmillan.

Wiener, M. J. (1990). *Reconstructing the Criminal: Culture, Law, and Policy in England 1830-1914.* Cambridge University Press.

Zedner, L. (1991). *Women, Crime and Custody in Victorian England.* Clarendon Press.

CHAPTER 5:
FAILURE IN EDUCATION:
KNOWING WHAT YOU *DON'T* KNOW

Susan Greenberg

This chapter explores the role of failure in education, using the teaching of creative writing as an example of how important failure can be to learning and the creative process.

All writing that aims for originality and beauty has failure at its core. In true stories as well as fictional ones, creativity is about acting as a shaping consciousness; noticing things, imagining the ways they might be connected, and then communicating that to others. There is beauty in the story's shape alone, but even more beauty and pleasure if the story leaves spaces for the imagination, and asks questions about what the writer does and does not know. In the novel *The Sorrows of an American*, Siri Hustvedt wrote: 'Words create the anatomy of a story, but within that story there are openings that can't be closed.' When stories do not provide those openings, they disappoint. When the stories are about real people, places and events, the disappointment has real consequences. After the 2008 recession, when the public complained that the media had failed to raise the alarm, thoughtful journalists responded that the prevailing demand for certainty left little room for discussion. 'The media tend to deal with good vs. bad,' commented the BBC's Evan Davies at a public debate in February 2009. 'We need more room for the discussion of what is "possible".'

Perhaps we should abandon the language of policymaking, social constructivism and 'best practice', and look instead to the language of poetics. The term has come to refer to the principles behind the written art form, but originally it referred to any cultural artefact, distinct from nature. Poetics, which derives from the Greek root *poiein*, 'to make', gives us permission to attend to the process rather than the finished object. Thus a single word holds within itself a whole world of incompleteness, and hence imagination.

So, for example, Creative Writing Professor Robert Sheppard speaks of poetics as an alternative to 'totalising theories', models, manifestos or explanations. Instead, he says, it offers 'a speculative, writerly discourse' of self-organising that allows the working out of difficult ideas about how something is to be made, and has 'built into it an awareness of the mobility of text, about what hasn't yet been written'. And the intellectual historian Richard Kearney, in his rich survey *The Wake of Imagination*, offers a vision of a 'poetics of the possible'; a reinterpretation of pre-modern, modern and post-modern ways of understanding imagination that leaves behind parody and pastiche and rediscovers 'the emancipatory practice of imagining alternative horizons of existence'.

THE CLASSROOM EXPERIENCE

The provisional nature of a text is one of the most important things that a new writer can learn, and sometimes one of the hardest things to teach. The very idea of teaching writing remains controversial, especially in the setting of higher education. As Paul Dawson charts in *Creative Writing and the New Humanities*, we still struggle with a strain of Romanticism that depicts creativity as synonymous with effortless 'inspiration'. John Keats wrote, 'If poetry comes not as naturally as the leaves to a tree, it had better not come at all,' and creativity is often seen as the direct expression of unconscious thoughts rather than something deliberately constructed. In contrast, Edgar Allen Poe summed up an alternative practitioner's view, when he wrote that he did not have 'the least difficulty in recalling to mind the progressive steps of any of my compositions'. Writing seems to suffer more from this prejudice than other arts; the painter or musician is not generally scorned for undertaking formal study. Of course the spark of creativity must come from within, but people can and do learn from others. To teach writing is to acknowledge the labour, and the conscious desire, involved in discovering one's material and crafting it to produce particular effects. Creativity depends not just on inspiration, but also on extensive experience and apprenticeship.

When any practice is brought into the academy, there is always a tension between professional and academic paradigms. And with formal assessment also comes the tension between the tutor as coach and mentor, and the tutor as judge. Overall, the marking criteria are defined in a way that allows the two to overlap: a work that gains a high grade in a degree programme is usually also something of publishable quality. But in assessment one is looking not just at how well the work measures up to professional standards, but also at what is being learnt. In addition, a grade can only offer a snapshot in time, rather than a definitive statement about a work's potential, were it to go through further drafts.

The aim of a writing course, like most practice-based subjects, is typically to help students develop a sense of what is possible, and understand the choices that arise along the way. One is looking at the text not just as a final product, but as something in the state of *becoming*. Practice embraces not just the work of putting words on the page, but also the reflection, dreaming, preparation and research that comes before, and the waves of editing and revision that come after. It is *all* creative, all part of the process; what is left out is just as important as what is put in.

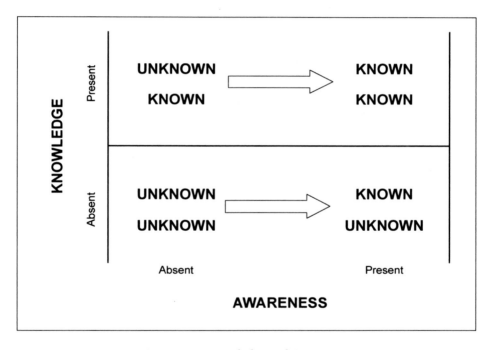

Figure 5-1: Knowledge and Awareness

There is a classic epistemological model that conceptualises four types of self-awareness about knowledge (Figure 5-1). A teacher will usually try to establish how much people already know (known knowns) and help them learn about the things that they know they don't know (known unknowns). But the teacher can go further, helping people identify the things they know only tacitly (unknown knowns) and the problems or choices whose existence they have never even suspected (unknown unknowns). You could say that the learning experience is a success if the student realises, by the end of the course, just how much she or he really does not know. In writing courses, the more students are aware of all four kinds of knowledge, the more likely they are to find things in their text at some stage that they consider 'wrong' and want to change. This awareness of the distance between what is, and what could be, is arguably the engine that drives the writer's imaginative powers. As Thomas Mann, the novelist and Nobel laureate, famously put it: 'A writer is somebody for whom writing is more difficult than it is for other people.'

In epistemology, knowledge is commonly described as developing in three stages. The first is **knowing that** – for example, that there is an eight-point story arc in drama, or that almost all forms of writing require some kind of research. The next is **knowing how** – knowing the principles involved in using that knowledge. The third is **being able** – the ability to put the principles into practice, using the skills associated with it. In a practice-based discipline, this involves learning not just a set body of knowledge, but a whole decision-making process, and adapting these to changing circumstances. So theory alone is not enough – one can only learn by doing. But practice alone (the thrown-into-the-deep-end approach of many entry-level jobs) is not enough either; reflection and feedback is needed to help put the action into a wider context.

If the aim of teaching in general is to help people realise fully the extent of what they *don't* know, the aim of reflective practice is to build on that new knowledge of ignorance. The student now 'knows that' her or his text needs more work, and wants to 'know how' to make it better. She or he also understands that even this will not be enough; progress from 'knowing how' to 'being able' will only come through constant practice.

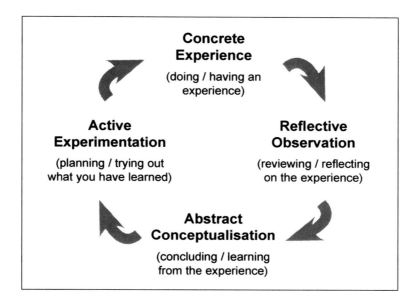

Figure 5-2: Kolb's learning cycle

This is where David Kolb's idea of the ***experiential learning cycle*** comes in (Figure 5-2). Here one moves from *concrete experience* (carrying out a core skill) to *reflective observation* (talking or writing about doing it), *abstract conceptualisation* or theory-building (the effect of reflection on how you do it) and then *active experimentation* and a repetition of experience. This process allows practice to be reflected on, rationalised, and presented in a way that traces the reasoning used, so that other people can recognise it and accept it as legitimate. It also allows theory to be tested so that concepts are continuously modified by experience. The influence works in both directions: practice is subjected to theoretical or contextual scrutiny, but theory is also tested against practice, so that it remains able to help explain, understand, predict or change that practice.

Kolb's educational theories are complemented by Donald Schön, who argues that professionals do not simply maintain an expert body of knowledge and retrieve it when needed: rather, they constantly engage with their practice, through actions underpinned by intrinsic intellectual processes, creating solutions appropriate to the specific context of a problem. That is why it is hard for a professional to instruct a novice simply by describing or showing any procedures, rules and theories.

Schön goes on to suggest the creation of a 'reflective practicum' at the centre of the school, to create a bridge between the worlds of practice and the academy. This approach is inspired by the studio model of traditional art schools, which emphasise coaching and learning-by-doing. Explicit theory is still important, as a way of providing meaning to the experience and framing questions. But practice is highly valued as something that draws deeply on our intelligence, experience and powers of critical reflection. The reflective practicum is all about providing a safe space to make mistakes, away from the immediate pressures of the workplace. It is a model that explicitly allows for failure as an integral part of learning.

CRITICAL REFLECTION – LEARNING FROM FAILURE

If we test this theory by its own criteria, we have to ask: how does it work in practice? In particular, in the setting of formal education, how does one assess the extent to which a student has engaged in the process of reflective practice? The answer, in the UK at any rate, is something called the critical reflection essay; also known as the reflective journal or critical commentary. This assignment allows the process behind the practice to be documented, separately from the creative work itself. In postgraduate degrees, where there is a higher level of engagement with theory, the essay also demonstrates the 'research-equivalent' activity required at that level. In the essay, the student is showing critical, analytical skills by using his or her own work as an object of study. The essay analyses the choices made during the writing of the creative work and makes explicit what would otherwise remain tacit. It can provide a statement of intent, against which the success of the work is measured. It also provides a way to assess evidence of learning, not just the 'output' or product of learning. It is a way of squaring the professional and educational process by getting marks for admitting mistakes, acknowledging the things one has *not* done, and exploring how one might do things differently next time.

The comments made in such essays show that most students do learn from practice, even if the quality of the assessed 'output' – the final submitted text – is not as high as it could be. Most importantly, essays often register a new awareness of previously 'unknown unknowns'; it is common for people to acknowledge the time taken for the experience to be digested, saying that they now look at the form of writing being explored 'with different eyes'. Formal assessment is therefore, inevitably, a snapshot taken before the picture is fully developed.

The critical reflection essay is not easy to write. This is partly because it is usually very different from the types of assessment people have encountered before, and partly because it runs so much against the prevailing cultural tide. It is hard for people to switch from highlighting their successes, in an 'onwards and upwards' narrative, to exploring their mistakes. Often they are suspicious when they hear that this is not only permissible but desirable.

Many commentators – more expert, articulate or higher placed than me – have already noted a crippling level of instrumentality in the education system and beyond, whereby things must be 'useful' if they are to be considered important, and there is a 'right' answer to everything. The paradox is that the stance 'I will do this, in order to get that' often makes achievement of a goal more elusive; those who do best are usually those who ask the most questions, and tolerate the most doubt.

The lack of practice that many people have in dealing with uncertainty also lays them open to huge anxiety about engagement with others, especially if those 'others' are different in some way. As a result, in the higher education setting, responses to other people's work can go from one extreme to the other; either the uncritical reproduction of their views, or their dismissal as entirely worthless. When constructive criticism and engagement is offered, it may not be recognised as something positive: the questioning of an idea is taken to mean that it is wrong. The response is often to drop the idea and replace it with an entirely new one, rather than working through the problem. This response is usually prompted by a lack of confidence rather than laziness: problems have been experienced as problematic, not something to be explored. Only with time does a person in that situation learn that any new idea, explored in turn, will not do away with the difficulty, but will soon produce a whole new set of problems, mistakes and doubts; and this is as it should be.

LIFE AS A REFLECTIVE PRACTICUM

The new media channels now populating our lives and imaginations, although not an unmixed blessing, open up interesting spaces for a poetics of the possible. In the past, awareness of text as something in a state of 'becoming' – rather than a final, finished product – was restricted mainly to the professional author, editor or publisher. Now, computer editing software and self-publishing interfaces make the process behind the scenes more obvious to a wider audience. At the same time, many people are looking for training that gives them professional communication skills, even if they do not end up using them in a professional setting. The main challenge is to explore this widening awareness without losing the acute insight and skill that comes from having experienced intermediaries such as editors, and without losing the potential of creativity that comes from resolution and polish.

The tensions now at play are illustrated by a web forum, 'The Bad Ideas Blog', established to note all those 'so-called bad ideas that *don't* make their way into books, whether as incomplete drafts, dropped chapters or simply deleted keywords'. The blog was set up in 2009 to accompany the launch of *Dreaming in Books* by Andrew Piper, who draws a parallel with the market for 'outtakes' or multiple versions in television and film. He writes: 'When you buy a book you never get the "what if". You get an extremely finished product. When you visit a website today, it can often feel like you *only* get the "what if". Online, nothing is ever finished [...] This project aims to bring together these two ways of writing into conversation with one another, to see what happens when the highly mediated form of the book is linked to the highly immediate form of the web.'

* * *

The model of reflective practice, and assessment by critical reflection essay, is in widespread use in all the practice-based disciplines that have grown up in higher education over the last decade or so. They are not perfect, but offer another way of thinking about success and failure. They depend on the existence of trust about how the expression of doubts or problems might be used, and such trust often does not exist. But it is still interesting to wonder where it might lead if we follow the insights that come from the teaching of writing, and other practices that make play with the imagination.

References / Further Reading

Dawson, P. (2005). *Creative Writing and the New Humanities*. London, UK: Routledge.

Hustvedt, S. (2008). *The Sorrows of an American*. London, UK: Sceptre.

Kearney, R. (2005). *The Wake of Imagination: Towards a Postmodern Culture*. London, UK: Routledge.

Kolb, D. (1984). *Experiential Learning: experience as the source of learning and development*. New Jersey, USA: Prentice-Hall.

Piper, A. (2009). *Dreaming in Books: The Making of the Bibliographic Imagination in the Romantic Age*. Chicago, USA: University of Chicago Press. Related blog: http://www.press.uchicago.edu/books/piper/index.epl?id=about [accessed March 2011].

Sheppard, R. (2008). 'Poetics as Conjecture and Provocation' in *New Writing: International Journal for the Practice and Theory of Creative Writing*. Vol. 5: 1, 2008. pp. 3-26.

Schon, D. A. (1983). *The Reflective Practitioner: How professionals think in action*. New York, USA: Basic Books.

CHAPTER 6:
FAILURE IN INDIVIDUALS AND SOCIETY
Robert Morrall & Kirsty Patterson

When written in Chinese, the word 'crisis' is composed of two characters –
one represents danger the other represents opportunity
John F. Kennedy, address, 12 April 1959

All individuals at times in their lives have moments of helplessness when they fail. It's a time when the 'physical wind' is knocked out of them. A time of sadness when the future looks negative and exerting effort is overwhelmingly difficult. For some people the recovery is very quick, with the symptoms of helplessness dissipating within hours. For others the helplessness can last for weeks or if the failure is important enough, for months or longer.
Robert Morrall, Learned Helplessness Grundtvig Project (2009)

The key concept for this Chapter is a condition known as 'learned helplessness' which is based on a theory developed by psychologist Martin Seligman (Seligman 1975). The theory helps to explain why people come to believe that they are powerless.

- Martin Seligman's initial experiments and the development of his theory of 'learned helplessness' began in 1967 at the University of Pennsylvania. At the time Seligman was interested in depression and it was by accident that he discovered how some outcomes of conditioning of dogs were the opposite of those predicted by the currently leading behaviourist school of psychology, as championed by B.F. Skinner (quoted in Seligman & Maier, S.F. 1967; Overmier & Seligman 1967).

LEARNED HELPLESSNESS

- Seligman demonstrated that people can be broken down by repeated experiences of failure to the point of extreme pessimism. Learned helplessness is the tendency by individuals to interpret past experiences and failures in such a way that when a similar situation arises they believe that they are powerless to do anything about it. The individual believes that any effort will be futile because past experiences have taught them that they are powerless to influence change.

- Seligman's research discovered that around one third of humans seem to be able to protect themselves from becoming helpless. These individuals will continue to try regardless of repeated failures and setbacks. However, the remaining two thirds of individuals remain vulnerable to failure. Through bitter life experiences most individuals will learn to feel powerless. These individuals believe that they have no control over their lives. This feeling is associated with depression and can adversely affect immune systems.

This chapter illustrates learned helplessness through four case studies and explores possible solutions where society can help. The case studies are drawn from the experience of Cementafuture, which is a not-for-profit social enterprise, operating as a business with social objectives to break down barriers to learning and recruitment in the construction sector. Cementafuture liaises with employers, candidates and project sponsors in order to provide work placement, and short and long-term employment opportunities. Candidates undertake a unique blend of bite-size training, personal support and work placement learning. A range of support is also available for those wishing to enter self-employment or start their own business. Cementafuture has developed the Destiny Project which, alongside other Cementafuture projects, aims to help both adults and young people create a positive vision in their lives, to have life goals and to teach them 'learned optimism', which for Seligman is a positive way to enhance the quality of life (Seligman 1991). An important component of Cementafuture is the Vision Journal. This is a tool used in its Cementafuture and Destiny projects. In a photo album a candidate is encouraged to display images of things they would like to achieve in life. They may be physical objects, lifestyle, learning or employment positions. It is a way to start firming up life goals that previously would have been abstract mental concepts to the individual. Vision Journals help practitioners to explore life goals with candidates and to start creating positive visions for the future. The aim is to create visions and life goals that leave behind the failures of the past.

- The Cementafuture Destiny Project works with young people who come from an offending background, or are at risk of offending. Typically these young people come from dysfunctional family backgrounds, are well known by the local police, and/or have contact with gang and drug cultures. School has been a negative experience and on leaving school (or being excluded), they drift into long term unemployment that reinforces their view of life as a pointless exercise in which they can achieve little.

Case Study 1 – Learner A

Referred by the police to the Destiny Project, Candidate A comes from an abusive childhood and broken family. He is a clever, young person, but has no direction in life, low self-esteem, low self worth, depression and had developed learned helplessness. Prior to joining the Destiny Project, he had been picked up several times by the police, although not arrested. On occasions he was staying away from home overnight and on one occasion ran away from home and slept rough in Luton. He lives in his father's home, which he shares with his stepmother and two young children from his father's second marriage. His recent life failures include being thrown out of college for not submitting work and difficulty with building relationships, which was compounded by the death of a friend. He arrived at the Destiny Project with a suspected broken thumb caused by a fight.

During the 16 years of his life he had faced a series of events that led to a feeling of failure:

- Break up of his family structure which left him with his natural mother in France.
- Abuse in his home life which created barriers with his natural mother.
- Frequently returning home to France having visited his father, only to find that his mother had moved house.
- The death of a close friend.
- Being thrown out of College.
- Being unable to find employment in a time of recession (Winter 2009-2010).
- Failure to respond to parental pressure to provide an income into his father's home.

In the early days of the project his attention was limited, however he undertook to create a Vision Journal, from which an interest in music and IT/graphics was discovered. He was mentored by a graphic designer, who spent time with him as a young role model. He has undertaken work placement activity (both painting and decorating and helping to organise a small conference) and has undertaken some NLP sessions.

In the first weeks he had two flare-ups where he lost his temper and stormed out of the building. Both occasions seemed to have been triggered by failed relationships and friends interfering in his life through comments on his Facebook page and by spreading rumours about his relationships. During this time he punched a hole through the fence at home.

But, on the basis of his general improvement and discussions with his father and stepmother, it was decided to invite him to a meeting in Gothenburg with another group of training organisations. He only decided to participate three hours before his flight left. However, for three days he behaved with respect, established a good rapport with the group and was considered to be a well behaved young man. This time away has been a turning point in his attitude and relationship with key staff members.

He has now started formal Skills for Life training and has achieved a Level 2 in numeracy and an Information Technology Qualification (ITQ). Originally it was difficult getting him up in the morning; now he will happily arrive for a 9am start and often has to be asked to leave at around 6 o'clock in the evening.

In March 2010 he helped organise a conference for which he dressed in a dinner jacket. During the conference he participated in an event where he sat and talked to the audience of 30 people about his experiences. This presentation was in front of the local MP, Chief Executive of the local council, deputy mayor and four members of the police.

He still has a long distance to travel. Learned helplessness is often used as a self defence mechanism, which supports a habit of giving up. In group sessions his learned helplessness can lead to disruptive and negative mind frames and he can isolate himself from the group.

He has been given a project to establish a social enterprise, run by young people, in event and conference management. The development of practical business skills has helped create a move towards 'learned optimism', but personalised support is required to help complete his personal journey.

FAILURE AND SOCIETY

- Failure is a great modern taboo. Our learning society and media is awash with materials/programmes on how to succeed, but not how to cope with failure. Failure can lead to learned helplessness, which in turn becomes a new form of exclusion (not replacing but overlaying existing exclusion), thus creating new and more complex patterns of inequality that are by their complexity harder to resolve.

- The Learned Helplessness Grundtvig Project is a transnational network of partners, in England, Portugal, Slovakia and Sweden, who share their experiences and good practices of working with extreme disadvantaged groups in their respective countries. (www.help-less.net)

- Whether one is considering offenders or older workers in England, young pregnant teenage girls in Portugal, Roma communities in Slovakia or marginalised migrant groups in Sweden, the challenge regarding helplessness is not only that it is 'learned' (after some failure), but that helplessness somehow can be acquired during the process of growing up in excluded (culturally, socially, etc.) communities.

- Simply, many individuals living in excluded localities generally feel helpless from the time they start to perceive the world around them. Thereafter, any attempt to improve their situation (secondary education, employment, etc.) encounters difficulties based not only upon objective reasons (for example in the case of employment – low education, low skills, no experiences, etc.), but also upon this psychological barrier, which obstructs a client from trying as well.

Case Study 2 – Roma in Slovakia

- Work by the Transnational Learned Helplessness Network partners in Slovakia has highlighted the fact that individuals in Roma communities in Eastern Slovakia develop learned helplessness through the embedded culture of expected failure within their local communities.

- One Roma community in Eastern Slovakia has a population of 4,400 of which in 2005 only 25 had employment. The community is based in a steep valley by a river that frequently floods and has resulted in several deaths. The housing is largely made of scrap wood and metal. A dozen new brick/block flats have been built by local residents with external financial support and have been allocated through a lottery based system to local families.

- On leaving the Roma community, the mud track road climbs the steep hill to link with the normal Slovak road system and to the local village, complete with a church and a shop that is inhabited solely by white non Roma Slovaks.

- When catching a local bus the Roma know which parts of the bus they are expected to sit in. Likewise they know which bars in the local town are Roma bars and which are not. Skin colour and poor dental condition often identify an individual as Roma. Their knowledge of Roma discrimination conditions the individual to expect certain responses in social situations, such as an expectation that Roma are lazy, not trust-worthy and will thieve from non-roma groups.

- Individuals in the Roma community take failure as their norm. They do not expect to gain employment or indeed to be able to move out of the community. Failure in the community has become a self-reinforcing cycle. From the moment of birth, children's development is shaped by the community's self-fulfilling prophecy of failure. The result is learned helplessness. Roma individuals consider that external organisations and employers will expect them to fail, so they tend to follow the path that is expected of them and, therefore, to fail.

- These Roma communities have learned to fail and individuals in the community do not expect to succeed in life. It is a big challenge for integration programmes working towards Roma social inclusion in both the wider Slovakian state and EU community as a whole.

- Roma communities are an example of learned helplessness in society, where failure in society conditions the future. Diminishing the causes of failure can be relatively easy to achieve through employment, new housing and social inclusion programmes. Embedded learned helplessness, however, acts as a barrier. The causes of the failure can be treated but, without tackling the learned helplessness embedded in the Roma community, these actions come to nothing. The approach has to be holistic, dealing with the causes of failure whilst supporting Roma to unpick their learned helplessness and move towards a sustainable learned optimism.

Learned helplessness can be considered in the following terms:

- *Giving up.* Through failure the individual or society has learned to fail. Failure for many is easier than success. It is a form of self-defence. By giving up, the individual or society abdicates having to consider change in the future. It allows them to remain in a comfort zone.

- *Denying the possibility of alternative options.* The individual will not accept that the future can be altered by making choices or choosing alternative options. They do not perceive that they have multiple options to choose from. The individual is unable to understand that there is no correlation between the way things appear to them and the way things actually are. Instead they choose a path of non contingency where they believe they know what the end result will be.

- *Believing: I have no control over the outcome.* In believing that past failures have conditioned the future and that future results will be the same as in the past, the individual or community becomes conditioned to the belief that whatever they do, the future will always be the same. That whatever action they take, ultimately they have no control over the future, that the future is pre-conditioned or 'set in stone'.

- *Resistance to future outcomes is futile.* The individual believes in their learned helplessness. They believe that all action is futile.

- *Believing one is incompetent.* Learned helplessness has become embedded and the individual or community has learned to fail. They believe that they have no option in life and will then take the line of least resistance, becoming passive or submissive to life's challenges.

Learned helplessness shows that the explanatory style of an individual is learned rather than inherited, and this theory fits well when looking at academic performance: the individual will sometimes deliberately fail to reinforce their belief in their own learned helplessness. An example of this is the author's own experiences with young college students who successfully undertake two-year BTEC National Diplomas, only to fail to submit their final assignment through a fear that successful completion will lead to opportunities in higher education or in work, which they believe they will fail at. Incomplete current research also suggests that learned helplessness is an important mechanism contributing to passive behaviour in older and unemployed people.

FAILURE AND LEARNED HELPLESSNESS IN AN AGEING POPULATION

- Learned helplessness is an issue facing our ageing population, where individuals are increasingly having to work longer and thus to continue to learn new skills. Reflection on past dreams, ideals and subsequent failures leads to learned helplessness and an inability to move forward to new opportunities, new learning and challenges in life. A greater shared understanding of learned helplessness, together with new tools and methodology, can provide a valuable and practical input to the educational challenge of an ageing population.

- Through helping to redefine 'failure' and a greater understanding of the impact of learned helplessness on the individual adult's engagement and development of skills and the project, Lifelong Learning, can considerably help with the engagement of hard to reach groups.

- There is a need for the development of new tools and methodologies to tackle barriers created through failure and learned helplessness, and to help reduce the impact of failure in the future.

Case Study 3 – The Older Worker

- John was an older worker who had been constantly employed in the construction sector throughout his life. At the age of 50 he was made unemployed. This failure in his life had a dramatic effect on him from which he was unable to recover. The failure led to a long period of unemployment caused by John's learned helplessness. John felt victimised by the events and powerless to change anything. He felt that he no longer had skills to offer and this led to depression and a self-fulfilling downward cycle.

- John undertook a 12-week programme with Cementafuture consisting of basic craft skills, social incubation support and action learning in the community.

- Social Incubation is a methodology developed by Cementafuture and the Seirens transnational network funded under the EU Equal programme. In simple terms Social Incubation is a process supporting disadvantaged individuals in participating in society and Promoting Citizenship is their empowerment within society.

- A more precise definition of Social Incubation is 'a short-term process in a tolerant, flexible and friendly atmosphere that inspires hope and success through mentoring person driven processes, cycles of support and valuing and respect of the individual in order to encourage and empower individuals as citizens in society'. (Seirens Network – 2006)

- Encouraged by his engagement in the holistic programme, John started applying for jobs and quickly secured one on a construction site.

- The job only lasted a few weeks and then John was again unemployed. This time, however, the failure did not cause John to sink into learned helplessness as he had learned that he had a positive place in society and that there would be other opportunities in the future.

- John had developed 'learned optimism' and thus had begun to feel empowered in his life. He no longer considered his past a failure to dwell on and condition his future. John instead had developed a fundamentally different belief system and now considered that his life was not controlled by fate. By taking an optimistic stance John now keeps trying even though times are difficult. When faced with problems that cannot be solved, John is now more likely to reframe the situation to enable the best possible outcome.

FAILURE, ABUSE AND SOCIAL PROBLEMS

- Learned helplessness can be seen as a coping mechanism some people employ in order to survive difficult or abusive circumstances. An abused child or spouse may eventually learn to remain passive and compliant at the hands of his or her abuser, since efforts to fight back or escape appear futile. Even if an opportunity to report or escape the abuse arises, many victims of long-term abuse choose to remain in the relationship because of learned helplessness.

- Child abuse by neglect can be a manifestation of learned helplessness: when parents believe they are incapable of stopping an infant's crying, they may simply give up trying to do anything for the child.

- Another example in social settings involves loneliness and shyness. Individuals who are extremely shy, passive, anxious or depressed may learn helplessness to offer stable explanations for unpleasant social experiences. However, these individuals who demonstrate helplessness in social settings may be viewed poorly by others, thus resulting in a situation that reinforces the problematic thinking.

- Social problems resulting from failure and learned helplessness seem unavoidable; however, learned helplessness can be minimised by 'immunisation' and potentially reversed by therapy. People can be immunised against the perception that failure in events are uncontrollable, by increasing their awareness of previous positive experiences. Support for the individual can instruct in the area of contingency, bolster people's self esteem and help to develop learned optimism.

Case Study 4 - Learner B

Referred by the police to the Destiny Project, this candidate had recently spent five weeks in a high security prison. Over the preceding five years he had never been outside of his town apart from his prison sentence. The candidate had a criminal background, past drug abuse issues, a very short attention span and many unresolved issues in his life.

The candidate had embedded learned helplessness following previous failures in his life, including his time in prison. This learned helplessness has prevented the candidate in achieving his potential in society. In fact learned helplessness had directed his life into a negative direction.

Since he joined the project he has put together a Vision Journal and has had NLP sessions.

The candidate has undertaken a range of work placement activities including painting and decorating, work in a pallet yard and assisted in evening training sessions undertaken by Cementafuture to external clients. Also, he has started Skills for Life training and tests.

To give a flavour of his situation, the following is one day in his life in February 2010:

- He was on a bus to be in the Cementafuture offices for 9am, when he was set upon. Somebody grabbed him round the throat and shook him hard.

- He went to the police station to give a statement where he was kept for four hours.

- On leaving the police station around midday, he spent the remainder of the day working in the Cementafuture offices, even though he was considerably shaken.

- He left Cementafuture late afternoon, only to be set upon in the town centre by a group of youths, who inflicted a head wound, which landed him in hospital.

- On release from hospital in the early evening, he came back to the offices and assisted in the delivery of some external training, even though he had stitches in his forehead.

- He ended his day having an evening meal with members of the staff team.

The candidate had learned to fail in life. To him these events were the norm, he had developed learned helplessness through life's previous failures. These failures had been created through:

- Childhood and family life
- School
- Local community
- Big events in his life

It was decided to try and give him a break, different surroundings and an opportunity for work placement outside of his local town. To this end a work placement with a building company was secured for two weeks with accommodation.

Leaving for the placement, his mother was in tears saying it was the first time in his life he had ever done anything positive.

Helping to break the cycle of learned helplessness, leaving the failures of the past behind and moving forward to a position of learned optimism has empowered the candidate to take ownership of his life and to move forward in a positive way.

There are still many barriers for him to cross such as financial literacy and dealing with a drug issue, but his frame of mind is now positive to creating solutions and not letting past failure dictate the future.

SUMMARY

You reach a fork in the road where you make a decision.
You're either going to be a victim and live a life certainly not to
its fullest,
or you're going to choose this huge opportunity for growth

Ute Lawrence

Failure is a great modern taboo through which individuals feel they have lost the struggle and learn to become helpless, becoming passive and complacent, with their ability to control future events distorted.

When misfortune happens in life we tend to consider it as bad. Whether the failure suffered is financial loss, a business or career disappointment, an accident or health problem, the common response is 'Why me? What did I ever do to deserve this?'

Recognising learned helplessness and its linkage to past failure gives practitioners and policy-makers the opportunity to tackle long standing challenges in society that directly affect social cohesion and economic development. In order for society to develop and grow, individuals need to participate to their fullest extent. Learned helplessless stops individuals and communities from developing to their optimum. Learned helplessness results in:

- Failure to learn at school or in later life, resulting in low skills and achievement.

- Failure to engage in sustainable employment, resulting in dependency on the welfare state.

- Failure to build safe communities. Offenders believe that their past conditions their future and thus they reoffend – 80% of adult offenders reoffend within two years and 70% of young offenders within one year.

These failures are a cost to society because they create generations of wasted youth, add to the cost of the welfare state and have a direct impact on safety in communities. Society needs skilled labour to support businesses in order to compete in a world market place.

Allowing holistic approaches both at school and in the labour market would be a good starting point for preventative measures. A valuable contribution would be the development of a 'Personalisation Agenda' where actions are targeted at the needs of the individual and not solely at a group, and where delivery organisations are encouraged to work together to offer seamless, rolling holistic programmes for individuals who have experienced failure in their lives and have been unable to recover within a short timeframe. So often the solutions offered after failure are not holistic approaches, but compartmentalised to the expertise of the delivery organisation.

Failure offers both the individual and, indeed, society the opportunity to 'draw a line in the sand', to learn from the mistakes made and to open new doors for the future. Failure can be a positive turning point in an individual's life. It should be viewed not as something that holds the individual back but as an opportunity to follow a new path in life, to be able to rise to new heights, and to create and experience new dreams.

> *When the Gods choose to punish us,*
> *They merely answer our prayers.*
> Oscar Wilde

References

Overmier, J. B. and Seligman, M.E.P. (1967). 'Effects of inescapable shock upon subsequent escape and avoidance responding'. *Journal of Comparative and Physiological Psychology*, 63, 28–33.

Seligman, M. E. P. (1975). *Helplessness: On Depression, Development, and Death.* San Francisco: W.H. Freeman.

Seligman, M. E. P. (1991). *Learned Optimism: How to Change Your Mind and Your Life.* New York: Knopf.

Seligman, M.E.P. and Maier, S.F. (1967). 'Failure to escape traumatic shock'. *Journal of Experimental Psychology*, 74, 1–9.

CHAPTER 7:
LIFE EVENTS FAILURE
Christopher Knell

Life in its very nature is unpredictable. Everyday events occur that impact upon our lives. Will the train be late so I miss that job interview? Will I be involved in an accident, so that the job interview no longer matters to me? To some extent we can control what happens in our education, in our career, in our personal lives. But what happens when failure is thrust upon us? What happens when you think life is finally ticking along smoothly and disaster strikes, and how do we recover and grow from that experience?

Everyone who reads this chapter will have many examples of how they have experienced 'life events failure', which I define as 'failure which is imposed by a life-changing event outside our control'. Some of those experiences will have had more serious impacts than others but, irrespective of the impact, most of us have never given any real consideration to how they have affected our lives in the long term. By considering how we have all experienced life events failure, we can develop our understanding of how failure, in its myriad of forms, affects the different aspects of our lives and, perhaps more importantly, how failure in one area directly impacts upon all others.

As we walk through this subject together I will draw examples from two incidents. The first is my own experience of a serious accident I was involved in as a child. The second example is the 7th July 2005 bombings on the London public transport network.

PERSONAL LIFE EVENT EXAMPLE

The notable example of life events failure in my own life was an accident I was involved in when I was 12. On a September afternoon in 1993, I was cycling around the back roads of the small town in which I grew up, enjoying the last of the long summer evenings. The details are a little unclear but, at some point, a car came around a corner too fast and, as best as anyone can piece together, knocked me off my bike and then, amazingly enough, reversed back over me in order to park on the owner's drive.

I say it's all a little unclear as no one witnessed the accident and my first memory in life was waking up on a hospital trolley days later and watching the neon lights in the ceiling flash past as I was taken down for another CAT scan. To this day I don't remember anything before that moment. I often joke that I'm effectively only 16 years old, usually as an excuse for my sometimes childish sense of humour.

In the weeks that followed the accident I met my parents for the first time, I read my first book, and slowly recovered from my injuries. It was many months before I returned to school, and many years before my family and I truly understood how much of my memory was lost to me. It wasn't until I was 17 that I turned to my parents and said, 'You do realise when the nurse told me "Your parents are here" I just accepted that it was true, but I didn't know who you were'. Today I work as a trustee for Headway East London, a wonderful charity that supports brain injury survivors, and I do this in no small part because I realise how lucky I am. Besides my memory loss I have had no lasting repercussions, and being a young man when it happened I think it was easier to bounce back.

Looking at this in the context of life events failure it's clear that my accident created failure in other aspects of my life. My education had a setback because I had to relearn a lot of information, and if I had been older it would have equally caused failure in my career. It also caused failure in my personal relationships with friends and family. My parents insist to this day that I had terrible mood swings during my recovery, but what my friends noticed for several years was a relative immaturity in my social interactions, possibly through 'lack of experience' due to the memory loss. Looking back now, 16 years on from the accident, how did the experience shape me as an individual, and has my reaction been a positive one for me?

I finished school at the same time as my peers and with reasonable grades that were above average perhaps but nothing spectacular. In itself I consider this an achievement given how some things, like logical reasoning, remained with me, but the detail and the knowledge was lost with my memory. I left school and knew I wanted to become an accountant but couldn't find my motivation in life; like many people I tried my hand at University, found it wasn't for me and dropped out. Almost by chance I got a job in a low level administrative role in local government and developed a passion for my work. Not only was I earning the money to pay my way in life but I could also make a difference to society in my own small way.

Over the years I worked my way up within local government, studying accountancy and working for the voluntary sector in my free time. Today, among other things, I'm a Senior Principal Accountant in adult social care and a Trustee of Headway East London. I work hard, sometimes too hard, but I have a real passion for my work and take satisfaction in the knowledge that my work has a positive impact on other people's lives.

The unanswerable questions are these: Would I have pushed myself so hard if, in my teenage years, I hadn't had to do so to catch up with my peers? Or would I have accepted a slower pace of life, and perhaps a better work-life balance? Would I have focused my career in the public and charitable sectors, or taken a more lucrative role in the private sector? We will never know the answer to these questions but it's in asking them that we can endeavour to better understand ourselves and hopefully have more positive reactions to the life events failures that we have yet to experience.

PUBLIC LIFE EVENT EXAMPLE

The second example I'm using in looking at life events failure is the bombings of the public transport network in London on 7th July 2005, known colloquially as '7/7'. I have decided to use this example as it's one that is widely known about and had a massive impact, yet is rarely thought about in relation to how it has affected people across society.

The 7/7 London bombings were a series of four coordinated suicide attacks during the busy morning rush hour for London's commuters. Three bombs were set off on London Underground trains and a fourth on a bus. The first explosion happened at 8.50am on that fateful morning and by 9.19am a code amber alert was issued and all public transport across London was shut down. 56 people tragically lost their lives and around 700 more were injured.

I remember watching, from the live news feed and from my office window, the stereotypical British reaction happening in reality, as literally millions of people made the long walk home in near silence. The attack was explained away by the media as a protest at Britain's involvement in the controversial Iraq War. A memorial stands in London's Hyde Park to the 56 people who died that day, but today, for most people, it's simply another memorial to another footnote in another person's history.

I would never try to sum up the enormity of this event or the impacts it had upon the individual lives it touched, but in trying to understand such impacts we can better understand events of a similar scale elsewhere and how we might react should the worst happen and were we to become involved in such an incident. The question is how it impacted on people at the time of the event and whether it has affected their career or their social lives in the longer term. Would the 7/7 event make you more risk-averse, perhaps thinking twice about using public transport, for example?

DIMENSIONALITY AND THE COLLECTIVE EXPERIENCE

There is a clear dimensionality to the impact of life events failure on different people, which the example of 7/7 demonstrates so well. By dimensionality I refer to the differences in experience, severity and impact to the individuals and societies it affected. These are shown in Figure 7-1 as three dimensions.

Figure 7-1: Dimensions of life events failure impact

The *experience* of an event radiates out *from the individual to the collective*. In the case of 7/7 there was a relatively large number of individuals who directly experienced the bombing. Then there are the thousands who were on the London transport network at the time, who may not have been physically injured but were on the trains, buses or stations when it happened. Then there are the millions of Londoners and commuters who were watching the news or having to make the long walk home, not knowing if more bombs were to follow, perhaps reassured but also unnerved by the then unusual site of armed police on London's streets. And finally there were societies, both British and those around the world, worried for loved ones or simply compassionate for their fellow man. The sheer volume of condolence books and tributes given by a myriad of societies around the world is heart warming to any Londoner who lived through that experience.

Where were you when 7/7 occurred? Were you there on the train when one of the bombs exploded, or several thousand miles away in another country watching it on the news? How did you react to the event, and have you considered how your reaction might have changed if your experience of the event was more individual or more collective?

In the same way that the experience of a life event radiates out from the individual to the collective, so does the *severity* often radiate out *from profound to mild*. Those people at the heart of 7/7 who directly experienced the atrocity would undoubtedly have had the most profound experience. This is, perhaps, followed by those who, on Monday 11th July, had to get back on the train or bus into work, probably in stony silence, eyes darting about looking for 'suspicious looking characters' and unattended bags. Those further removed generally experienced progressively milder reactions as the reports made international news and as over time there were no repeat bombings or incidents closer to their loved ones.

It's typical to think that the individual at the heart of an incident must have the most profound impact while at the other end of the spectrum the collective must have the mildest impact. While on the whole this is the case and in generalising I have come to this conclusion, life events failure is about you as an individual, and the severity of the impact upon the individual is defined as much upon their past experience as it is to their proximity to the incident. New Yorkers, with 11th September still fresh in their minds, would no doubt have had a more profound reaction to the

London bombing than those living closer to London but whose cities had never had the misfortune of being the target of terrorist atrocities.

Finally, but no less importantly, is the dimension of the *impact type* of a life event, *from physiological to psychological*. As with the examples above, and often in conjunction with them, those closest to the incident are more likely to have physiological impacts whereas those further removed from the incident are more likely to have psychological impacts. Of the three dimensions this is by far the most interesting when considering the impacts of life events failure. It's far too easy to see the physiological and to brush over the psychological.

The physiological impact is significant and should not be underplayed, after all 56 people tragically lost their lives on 7/7 and around 700 hundred walking wounded received injuries ranging from life threatening to comparatively minor. We will explore further on in this chapter how these injuries, both physiological and psychological, can significantly change our abilities. We should not imagine that those impacts are mutually exclusive. Some individuals may have profound physiological injuries but mild or even no psychological impact, while others will certainly have no physiological injury but quite profound psychological impacts.

We do however have very little control over how the physiological impacts upon us; if we are unfortunate enough to experience such an incident of life events failure then it is thrust upon us. While never underestimating the difficulty of doing so, it is possible for us as individuals to influence the psychological effect. Immediately after 7/7 the survivors were offered counselling, with many businesses in London providing counselling for their staff, including those based outside of London but who had colleagues, friends and loved ones in the city. In the months and years that followed there was an outpouring of grief around the world as many nations showed their solidarity by mass signing of condolence books at embassies, holding a minute's silence and other acts of compassion. For those of us in London thousands attended remembrance services all over the city on the first anniversary, in itself a step towards us as individuals dealing with the psychological impacts of the incident and moving forwards.

The physiological can prevent us from doing some things we previously could, or can make it that much more difficult. For example, for wheelchair enabled 7/7 survivors getting back on public transport as their recovery progressed and they went about their lives. The psychological effects also prevent people doing things; there was an understandable anxiety for many getting back on public transport after what had happened. In the years that followed 7/7 the media reported on the psychological dread risk affect. Simply put, this was the understandable fear of repeat bombings that led to many people ditching public transport and taking up cycling instead. A sad result of this has been a significant rise in cycling injuries. Some sources place around a 20% increase in cycling injuries in the years following the incident, compared to the period immediately before 7/7.

If you were to look at the available information on the numbers of journeys and the volume of injuries sustained it would be perfectly logical to reach the conclusion that public transport is still the safest way to get about London. But would any of us really think less of someone who made the decision to cycle about town instead of taking public transport after such an event?

DIMENSIONALITY AND THE INDIVIDUAL EXPERIENCE

It is possible to take the example of dimensionality above, with its three axes of experience, severity and impact, and apply it to almost any incidence of life events failure. Indeed I encourage you to do this with your own experiences and consider which elements of your reaction you are happy with and which you'd like to change.

Going back to my own experience of life events failure in the form of the accident I had when I was 12, it's relatively easy to apply the dimensionality model and see how it radiates out, but then with all things it gets easier to judge an event impartially the further we get from it. To quote the British playwright Alan Bennett: *'There is nothing so remote as the recent past.'*

The experience of the accident was very individual. It affected me and the driver of the car at its focal point. Radiating out from this it was a significant experience for my family and closest friends, less so for school friends, then acquaintances, and barely registered in the consciousness of the local community. Similarly, while the severity was most profound for the driver and me, it was still very profound for my family but quickly and understandably tapered away to nothingness for friends, acquaintances and the local community. Finally the impact was physiologically profound for me as I was badly injured and physiologically mild for the driver, whereas the psychological impact was much more broadly spread with both the driver and me, and our respective families and friends, feeling the impact over the months and years as we recovered and put the experience behind us.

When we experience failure it affects our capabilities and the things that we can achieve in life. We each have our comfort zone within which we operate, depicted by the inner circle in the illustrations below. In our comfort zone we can achieve any outcome we set our mind to, whether that be in our career, our education, our family or indeed any other aspect of our lives. It is natural and I would argue healthy to want to push ourselves to move outside of our comfort zone. This might take the form of going for a promotion at work, studying for a new qualification, entering into a new relationship and so forth. Sometimes by pushing ourselves we fail and we have the choice either to accept that failure, and move back into our comfort zone, or to try again until we succeed, thereby expanding our comfort zone. This is shown in the left-hand part of Figure 7-2 by the expansion of that circle as we fail, learn, and go on to succeed – and in doing so improve our capabilities. You will have seen similar arguments elsewhere in this book in different settings.

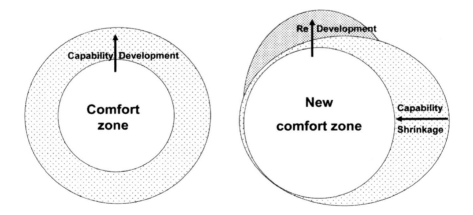

Figure 7-2: Changing comfort zones

This relates specifically to life events failure because sometimes an incident changes our capabilities and it shrinks our comfort zone, through loss of capability due to physiological or psychological changes. This is depicted by the right-hand part of Figure 7-2. Sometimes, through support or perseverance, we can regain those lost capabilities, but equally sometimes we need to have the strength of character to accept that our capabilities have changed. But this change does not have to stop our growth as individuals.

Imagine for a moment you were involved in an accident similar to my own experience of life events failure and have lost a significant segment of your memory. Or that you were involved in an incident such as 7/7 and the physiological or psychological impact left you unable to do something that you were once capable of doing. In the context of one's career this could very easily mean you are no longer able to do the job you were doing, but that does not have to be the end of it. The loss of one ability presents an opportunity to refocus your attention in a different area. Many people who have experienced life events failure have seen significant changes in their life as they move away from doing things where they were once able or felt comfortably part of and instead do something different.

There are countless examples of people who were once dependent upon their physical prowess suffering injuries and refocusing their lives in new ways, perhaps taking an office job or becoming a coach for others in their field of expertise. In the case of people with a brain injury, some go on to work with other brain injury survivors to help them through the difficult transition, conscious of the individual way it manifests for each person. And in the example of 7/7, many survivors formed support groups, became motivational speakers or wrote about their experiences so that others might reflect upon them.

Of course until we have been through such an experience it is impossible for us to say for certain that we know how we would react, or even to say if we could exert any conscious control over our reactions. It is important to remember that no reaction is more or less valid, just individual. But perhaps in understanding our own reactions we can better understand ourselves and predict our future reactions to the challenges that life inevitably presents to us.

PERCEPTIONS OF LIFE EVENTS FAILURE

Many books have been written on 'what ifs', the counterfactual study of events past and present to try and understand how things could have been different. On a societal level this can cover everything, from *What if Hitler hadn't survived World War One: would World War Two still have happened?*

to – a 2010 example – *What if bankers had shunned repackaged mortgaged debt: would the Credit Crunch still have happened?* These books inevitably look at how change, often a small change in the life events of an individual, would have had wide ranging repercussions. Surely the more interesting question is not what would happen if that life event were changed, but rather what if the reaction to that event was different? Of course any such consideration is speculative for we shall never truly know. On an individual level if I as the author hadn't been in an accident as a child, how could my life be different and would I be writing this chapter on life events failure?

It's quite likely that as you have read through this chapter some of the points have resonated with you while others you may not fully agree with. That is undoubtedly the most interesting and, as an author, the most challenging thing about life events failure. It isn't clear cut and there isn't a rule book to follow. It's subjective and, most importantly, it's personal. In doing my research for this chapter I read many articles and spoke to several people about their own experiences and interpretations of failure. Interestingly enough it's in talking to those people who were the most sceptical about the concept of life events failure that I found the best ways of illustrating the problems with failure of all types and particularly the perceptions of failure.

The following statements demonstrate these varying perceptions:

- *'Experiencing a life event doesn't count as failure, it wasn't a test to be failed, it just happened.'*

Experiencing a life event doesn't mean you've failed. Usually these things are entirely by chance; if you were running 5 minutes earlier or later you might have missed that chance encounter all together. Instead life events failure is about recognising and understanding how a life event creates failure in other areas of your life. The different aspects of our lives, some of which have been explored in the other chapters of this book, all overlap with one another. Life is not made up of discrete areas that can be compartmentalised without impacting on the others, and that is why it is necessary to truly consider failure in each of those different aspects of life before we can begin to understand it.

- *'Failure is personal, being caught up in 7/7 wasn't personal, it happened to lots of us.'*

Failure is personal, or perhaps more precisely, our reactions to failure are personal. An event on the scale of 7/7 is anything but individual, because it affects many people, but it is very personal. Countless individuals were affected physiologically or psychologically but the attack was not targeted at any one individual. Each individual dealt with the incident in their own way. While their reactions may have borne some similarities to each other, those reactions were truly personal and that is why life events failure is such an important topic in understanding the overarching concept of failure.

- *'People fail in life, life doesn't fail them.'*

This is a powerful statement, and I'm sure most of us have felt that way about ourselves or someone else at one time or another. Personally one of my biggest disappointments with society is that, too often, we say it's not our fault that we were failed by someone or something else. We all fail at times and sometimes that failure is outside of our control such as when it is imposed by a life event. Experiencing failure, in any aspect of our life, does not make us a failure; it does not mean we have failed in life. Nor does life fail us, but it does throw challenges our way and failure is active not passive. How we respond to those challenges defines us as individuals, but it would be foolish for anyone to judge an individual and declare they have failed in life.

FINAL THOUGHTS

Earlier in the chapter I talked about my own experience of life events failure and how the events that occurred affected me and the people around me in different ways. I consider the long term outcome of that experience to be a positive one but I would never suggest that any reaction is wrong or bad. Our reactions to life events failure are individual and unique.

You may think 'This is interesting stuff, but where does it tell me how I'm supposed to respond to life events failure?' Well I'm afraid it doesn't. My intention is that by considering the events of our lives and our reactions to them, in the context of some of the themes I have identified here, we can each reach an outcome that we as individuals are happy with. Remember, the only person qualified to judge your reaction to your individual experiences of life events failure is possibly the harshest judge of them all – yourself.

CHAPTER 8:
FAILURE IN PROJECTS, PROGRAMMES & CORPORATE STRATEGY

Stephen Charters

Beauty is in the eye of the beholder, as the saying goes, and this applies equally to perspectives of failure. To adapt another saying, one man's failure is another man's lesson learned.

The concepts of the characteristics and dimensions of failure outlined in Chapter 2 show that perspectives of failure can vary. We can easily relate to this idea as individuals, but here I shall explore how these perspectives operate within organisations at levels above the individual and groups or teams, i.e. from projects and programmes, up to the highest level of corporate strategy. Failure or success at any one of these levels may not be perceived as such at another level. If we are serious about developing a more mature attitude to failure in general, we have to develop a wider perspective at all of these levels, and beyond them into society as a whole.

It should come as no surprise to find a chapter on projects in a book about failure. So-called 'failed' projects are one of the media's favourite targets when they are looking for a headline. From the Millennium Dome, through the new Wembley stadium, to Heathrow Terminal 5, many column-inches are devoted to describing what has gone wrong and seeking someone to blame. Successful projects that complete to time, budget and specification, and then actually work, are not newsworthy and so get little attention.

For example, St. Pancras station was completely redesigned, enlarged and modernised to accommodate the Eurostar train service, while maintaining existing rail and underground services. The full project is reported to have completed on time and within budget, yet I only recall seeing reports in the news about the project on the opening day of the Eurostar service, the media then moving on to something more interesting. There was no inquest into how it all went so smoothly and there were no interviews with passengers who didn't feel aggrieved.

If all we see are the negative sides of projects, it is no wonder that people feel that the UK has little competence and that nothing works properly.

Yet if we don't take risks and introduce change properly, our society will stagnate.

So here are a few headlines of my own that set the tone for this chapter.

NEW REVELATION – PROJECTS ARE RISKY AND MAY FAIL!

PROGRAMME ON-TRACK DESPITE PROJECT FAILURE – SHOCK!

FAILURES OVERCOME, AS RISK SUCCESSFULLY SPREAD ACROSS PORTFOLIO!

The problem as I see it is that, at least in the UK, we do not have an adequate language in general use that could help us to talk intelligently about risks. This chapter seeks to explain some of what that language might look like by describing some of the key characteristics of projects, programmes and corporations, how they are managed and how this relates to perceptions of failure. It is not intended to be a primer in project or risk management. Instead it seeks to offer a 'way in' to the subject, aimed at those readers who do not come across this type of language and thinking in their daily lives.

The aim is to provide the reader with an insight into the risky world of project, programme and corporate management, such that they will feel better equipped to challenge and interpret the way failure is reported in the media. If we are to break out of this negative stereotyping of anything that might fail, we need to be better informed about the risks involved at an early stage, about the likelihood of failure and what failure actually means.

What follows is based on generally available theories of corporate strategic planning, programme and project management, risk management and stakeholder analysis. Typical reference works are cited at the end of this chapter for those who are interested. However, this is by no means an exhaustive analysis, rather an overview based on personal observed experience. For the purpose of this chapter, here are a few definitions to assist any readers unfamiliar with these concepts.

PROJECT, PROGRAMME AND CORPORATE LEVELS OF RISK

Defining the project level

The UK Association for Project Management (APM) defines a project as 'a unique and transient endeavour undertaken to achieve a desired outcome'. So it is no wonder that projects may fail; they are risky. For a start they are unique, so by definition involve doing things that haven't been done before. They are transient, so they have a start and a finish. This means a project has to set up from scratch, often in an unfamiliar environment, with a team of people that may not have worked together before. Finally they deliver a desired outcome, which opens up more areas of risk: firstly involving the difficulty in defining what is desired and then the difficulty in delivering something that matches it; secondly in that the desired outcome implies some form of change – and change, as we all know, involves risk.

Projects do not exist in a vacuum. They operate within an environment and a hierarchy as described in Figure 8-1. Projects themselves also have a hierarchical organisation, called a Work Breakdown Structure (WBS), within which actual work is delivered by teams of individuals, utilising raw materials and equipment.

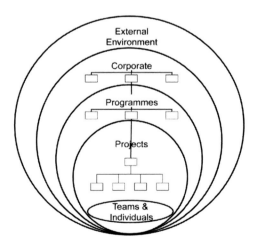

Figure 8-1: Levels of hierarchy

Defining the programme level

Working up Figure 8-1, 'The APM Body of Knowledge' defines programme management as 'the co-ordinated management of related projects, which may include business-related activities that, together, achieve a beneficial change of a strategic nature for an organisation'. Programmes therefore will encounter the same issues as projects, but with the additional complexity of managing one or more projects or other activity. However this can also mean that programmes have the ability to absorb the impact of problems with any one individual project. We shall explore this in more detail later in this chapter.

Corporate bodies will tend to deploy their strategy through the creation and management of programmes of work.   Therefore, typically, a programme is absolutely central to the success of the corporate body that launched it and that expects to benefit from its results.

Defining the corporate and external environment levels

Corporate bodies control one or more portfolios of projects, programmes and 'business as usual' activities to deliver their mission. In doing so they are answerable to, and have to deal with, a wide range of stakeholders in their external environment.

The concept of 'corporate body' used here encompasses not only commercial enterprises, but also the wide range of not-for-profit organisations, such as charities and government departments and agencies. Typically, corporate bodies will deliver products and services to meet a stated mission: commercial enterprises will seek to make a profit now and deliver increased profits in the future; not-for-profit organisations will seek to deliver a standard of service to their stakeholder group, while responsibly managing costs. Henceforth I shall use the term 'Value' to describe this overarching aim of any corporate body. Since their aim is usually to succeed in the future as well as the present, virtually all corporate bodies will seek to achieve significant improvement in their performance and capability over time. Many seek to achieve these improvements through deploying projects and programmes.

To complete the explanation of Figure 8-1, the External Environment covers the wide range of stakeholder groups that are affected by and/or influence the operation of corporate bodies. That includes the general public, pressure groups, regulators, government and other corporate bodies. This means that corporate bodies also have to pay attention to how they interact with a very varied environment, covering subjects such as community relations, environmental issues, ethical behaviour and regulatory compliance. For now I shall treat all these subjects under the general heading of Reputation and Compliance.

Although a simplification, one might differentiate the main perception of each level as follows:

- Projects focus on Delivery.
- Programmes focus on Benefits.
- Corporate bodies focus on Value, Reputation and Compliance.

Defining risk

Hand in hand with all of this activity is the concept of risk – the 'uncertainty that matters' that is associated with future events. Risks exist at different levels, i.e. project risk, programme risk and corporate risk. Success or failure will depend heavily on how well risks are identified in advance and managed at each of these levels.

One clear sign that risk is being taken into account is the existence of some contingency allowance for delays and/or additional costs. Another is that actions are being taken in advance, in anticipation of possible future events.

Risk, as defined in the modern standards on risk management, can have positive as well as negative effects. At first glance this may seem to run counter to normal usage, whereby risk is generally seen as negative. However, in reality one rarely takes a risk without a reason, and that reason is usually either seeing an opportunity or avoiding a greater threat. So the two concepts of threat and opportunity go hand in hand and, in practice, the process of identifying and managing threats and opportunities is, in essence, the same. You identify a threat or opportunity, decide what you want to do about it and then put in place actions to do something about it: typically, you either enhance or exploit an opportunity, or mitigate or avoid a threat.

In particular, as we move down the levels of the hierarchy, a decision to address a risk at one level often generates threats and opportunities at a lower level.

PERSPECTIVES OF FAILURE

We shall now look at perspectives of failure at each of these levels in more detail, interspersed with some examples drawn from recent UK project history. In describing these examples, and in the subsequent discussion, I am not offering an in-depth analysis of each, but am relying on generally available information drawn from press reports and personal anecdotes. Any consequent inaccuracies only serve to illustrate that we are dealing here with perceptions of failure, rather than a more balanced view of reality, which would be based on established and verifiable historical facts and analysis.

The project perspective of failure

The traditional focus of projects is on delivering their outcome within the constraints of time, cost and quality. 'Time' represents the deadline set for the project to deliver its outcome. 'Cost' is usually defined by working within a given budget or a fixed contract price and a target profit margin. 'Quality' represents the measurable outcome of the project in terms of what is to be achieved, which might include, for example, standards of workmanship. Some project management models include a fourth success criterion to represent Customer Satisfaction, covering elements outside measurable quality. These are sometimes shortened to 'QCDD':

- Quality (covering specification)
- Cost
- Delivery (i.e. time)
- Delight

Projects can tend to be rather tunnel-vision in their approach, focusing all effort on finishing as quickly as possible, while staying within their budget and while managing key aspects associated with whatever they are trying to deliver: aspects such as ensuring their output meets quality requirements and protecting people against risks associated with health and/or safety. Therefore a lot of effort needs to go into up-front definition of the scope and constraints of the project because, once it is launched, most project managers will drive hard to complete within that scope as soon as they can. Issues outside that scope will struggle to get a look-in.

One can understand why this approach is usually adopted. Time is usually of the essence in any case, but another enemy of a successful project is change, either in external environment or in scope and requirements. At the extreme, change can invalidate the whole concept of a project but, more commonly, change introduces significant costs and delays through the need for re-design and/or rework. Thus a fast-paced project reduces the risk of change by reducing the window of time in which it can happen.

This approach does have its drawbacks, especially in projects where the customer requirement is immature at the start. Customers can be very clear on what they do not want, once they see it. Unfortunately they may only realise this at the moment the project manager proudly hands over what he was told to produce, when they immediately see it was not what they really wanted.

The way in which projects are established and managed is characterised by a focus on time, cost, quality and (sometimes) delighting the customer. These are the factors that dominate the perception of success or failure at the project level.

However, if left to their own devices, such projects may lose sight of the external environment outside of their scope. Controlling this tendency is one of the main concerns of the programme level, which we shall cover later, but first I have included some reflections on the nature of the project perspective of failure using the example of the Millennium Dome.

Example 1: The London Millennium Dome
– the 'Greatest Show on Earth'

Ask anyone their opinion of the London Millennium Dome and they will probably define it as a failure. The Dome was intended to be the centrepiece of the UK's millennium celebrations but, in the event, it overspent its budget and was generally regarded as not meeting the goal set by the then Prime Minister Tony Blair to be the 'Greatest Show on Earth'. Visitor numbers were disappointing, with only 4.5 million paying visitors during 2000 as opposed to the projected 12 million. General feedback was that the exhibits within the Dome were unimpressive and the whole visitor experience did not live up to expectations. Sponsorship income was also significantly lower than expectations and it proved difficult to find a buyer for the site once the millennium exhibition was over. Therefore the project needed substantial additional funding from the Millennium Commission.

However, the construction of the Dome, in itself a challenging exercise, was completed on time, to budget and to specification. In addition, irrespective of what happened in 2000, the Dome is now a commercial success under new ownership and under its new name of the O2 Arena.

So as a construction project, it met its criteria of completing to time, cost and specification and the structure is still in use today. The larger project aimed at delighting the ultimate customer clearly failed, however. Specifically, the project associated with defining the exhibition did not appear to achieve satisfactory quality, and poor perceptions of the content of the Dome's exhibits led to low visitor numbers. The negative impacts on both profit and reputation meant that, at the programme level, the venture did not deliver the benefits and lost money. However, the larger programme also included a benefit driver related to the regeneration of the surrounding area, so the current success of the O2 Arena could indicate success in delivering that aspect of the benefit stream.

In the next section I will look at the programme level in more detail, while introducing another example to illustrate the differing perspectives of failure at project and programme level.

The programme perspective of failure

Sometimes a project can seem to be a failure but, on inspection, can demonstrate that it has done exactly what it was asked to do. The actual source of failure can therefore often lie more in the difficult problem of defining what had to be done, which is a programme-level responsibility.

A programme will generally inherit the overall perspectives of the corporate level but will tend to break each value driver into more detail, to describe more precisely the benefits specific to this programme. Some programmes will deliver value to the corporate body by developing new products or services, while others may do so by improving production methods to reduce costs. Some large programmes will set out to do a combination of both. The programme delivers these benefits via the co-ordinated deployment of a series of projects, possibly also utilising other non-project components.

Therefore a programme has to understand risks at the corporate level that are relevant to its success, to evaluate how these affect the programme and then to decide what to do about them. It then has to cascade benefits and risks to each of its projects such that, collectively, they deliver the overall aims of the programme while managing their share of the risks. This involves a close focus on communication and co-ordination.

To achieve this cascade, programmes have to ensure that their benefits are defined in terms that both relate to the value the corporate body is trying to achieve and are in terms that make sense to the project. Such benefits also have to be measurable and verifiable. Having done that, the programme must also ensure that these benefits are properly represented in the scope of each of its projects such that, taken together, they deliver the full benefits expected. So, in the example above of the Millennium Dome, the value from the aspect of urban regeneration has, in some way, to be reflected in the benefits that the area will gain by having a successful entertainment venue such as the Dome.

Another important aspect of benefits definition, and how it influences the scope of a project, relates to the implications of the full project life-cycle. For example, in the case of new product development projects, it is much more common nowadays to allow for the environmental impact of product disposal at the end of its working life.

Some apparent project failures may be more attributable to poor communication of the key risk drivers to the project by the programme. Sound programme management has to take account of the fact that the inevitable tunnel vision of each project can lead to a lack of concern for the wider benefit stream, and/or the various viewpoints of the external environment. As an example, programmes (and/or corporate bodies) have to ensure that over-enthusiastic project managers do not inadvertently upset the local community, damaging the corporate reputation. Also programmes, developed from a wider perspective over a range of projects, are well placed first to see common risks occurring across several projects and then to either ensure that all projects manage them or to manage some of them on behalf of the projects.

It is also at this programme level that most attention can be paid to how benefits and risks can be communicated across all stakeholder groups. If a programme pays enough attention to managing stakeholder expectations, it can have a significant effect on the final perception of success or failure. Communication activity also exists at the other levels as well, of course.

Apart from communication, programmes also have to pay a lot of attention to co-ordination and prioritisation in controlling the launch and delivery of the projects within the programme. Programmes that fail to co-ordinate their projects can be perceived as failures despite any individual project successes. For example, a programme to develop a new product range must work hard to ensure that new design ideas do not get out of step with the capability of existing production facilities; otherwise they may design products that are too expensive or impossible to produce.

Thus, at the programme level, the prime drivers of success are benefits (including future capability), reputation, compliance, communication of benefits and risks, and co-ordination. These, for me, are the factors that dominate the perception of success or failure at the programme level. This is illustrated by our second example, which allows us to reflect more on the project level and then move on to the programme level.

Example 2: Heathrow Terminal 5
– 'One of the World's Best'
Heathrow Terminal 5 was another major project that completed on-time and under budget, yet is again associated in the public mind with failure due to significant problems on its opening day in March 2008. Problems with baggage handling and security systems led to large passenger queues and delayed and cancelled flights. The negative publicity associated with the opening damaged the reputations of the two key stakeholders – British Airports Authority (BAA) and British Airways (BA) – as well as somewhat denting national pride.

Reflecting a little on the project level first, Terminal 5 had many characteristics that made it risky. Construction had to take place close to a motorway, a nature conservation area and at the end of two busy runways, without disrupting flights. A number of underground tunnels had to be completed early and these were completed ahead of schedule and well under budget. Many of the project management and contracting practices used at Terminal 5 are now being applied to the construction of the site for the 2012 London Olympics. So, as a 'megaproject' it nearly succeeded on all counts and, as at least one report points out, all new airports tend to have teething problems on opening, especially with baggage handling. This is, of course, no consolation to those who had their travel plans so disrupted in those early days.

At the programme level, this example tells us a lot about the importance of communication. Terminal 5 was saddled with a rather ambitious statement of its benefits. Shortly before the opening, BA was reported as saying 'The opening of Heathrow's Terminal 5 will change the way international travellers look at Britain and restore our principal airport to its rightful position as one of the world's best.' So, since we have already said that stakeholder communication is a vital element of programme management, we can now see that the perceived failure of the project is closely linked to the expectations set beforehand.

While on the subject of communication, a lot of the media coverage of the opening revealed that passengers at the terminal received very little information during the time of their delay, which greatly added to their dissatisfaction. This may have been unfair reporting, it is hard to say, but, if true, it would represent a failure against the criterion of Delight. This illustrates the axiom that even during a failure, you turn it into a success by the way you treat your customers while the failure is happening.

A year after the opening it could be argued that the terminal had met its vision, being fully operational and generally well liked by passengers using it. BA were able to report that 'Terminal 5 is now working, with over 20 million people having used it since it opened'. Customer feedback scores were good and BA achieved their best punctuality and baggage delivery standards for a decade. By simply removing the first three words of the BA statement quoted above ('The opening of...'), the expectations might have been set differently, by focusing on the eventual operational performance after any teething problems had been overcome.

Looking now at the co-ordination aspect of the programme level, the Terminal 5 development was a very large project in itself. However, it was only part of a larger programme to upgrade the other Heathrow terminals. Once BA had moved to Terminal 5, space was to be freed up at other terminals to start their refurbishment. We might therefore expect that any delay in this project would have had a knock-on effect on the follow-on refurbishment activity. However, if that risk was identified at the programme level and some contingency allowed, the whole programme would perhaps be able to recover without serious damage to the overall benefits.

From the co-ordination perspective one might argue that the handover from construction to the opening day seems to have suffered some failures at the programme level. However, it is probably too early to say whether the overall programme has failed. There is an indication of communication failure, based on the press reports of passenger experiences during the confusion in the opening days and on the expectations set prior to opening. However, that latter impact relates more to the corporate level, as we shall now explore.

The corporate perspective of failure

Any corporate body exists within an environment, where it has to seek to survive and prosper by delivering value to its prime stakeholders. In a business this is achieved by delivering shareholder value, which is in turn achieved by delivering goods and services to a customer-base while generating a profit now and increased profit in the future. Governments seek to deliver a wide range of services to their electorate (who effectively also form the customer-base) under a concept of value for money.

In theory at least, the way for all these corporate bodies to deliver value is to develop a strategy that matches core capability to market needs, both now and in the future. The corporate body can then deploy that strategy through two types of activity that, taken together, can be regarded as one or more portfolios.

- First, they have to put in place the resources and manage the 'business as usual' activities necessary to deliver existing products and services.

- Secondly, they initiate and deliver a series of projects and programmes to achieve some form of beneficial change over time.

To achieve change nearly always involves the launching of projects and programmes and this applies to perhaps a wider range of activity than some might expect. It will include: new product or service development, performance improvement, re-organisation or relocation, capital expenditure, mergers & acquisitions and expansion into new markets. The cost of these has to be met from within available sources of funding and resource, implying that some hard choices have to be made at corporate/ portfolio and programme level.

Such value-oriented activity is aimed at establishing a continually improving portfolio of products and services that meet customer needs and deliver a profitable and/or valuable return. While doing so, the corporate body has to ensure that it maintains its reputation and complies with legal, regulatory and ethical standards.

The whole process of developing corporate strategy also involves the consideration of the needs of a wide range of stakeholders in the business. The term stakeholder is a very useful one because it is so broad a concept. Stakeholders can be any group or individual with an interest in a corporation's activity. They typically include: Shareholders, Customers and Markets, Competitors, Staff, Suppliers, Government and Legal Frameworks. Just to complicate things, corporate bodies also have to take account of other bodies that may be influenced by their operations, such as the general public, pressure groups and, especially for national governments, other countries.

Each stakeholder group will have different perspectives and the relative importance of these can usually be measured in terms of levels of *power*, *interest* and *attitude*. How the company treats each stakeholder group will effectively determine the perceptions of success or failure of the organisation.

Failure in the management of the relationship with staff, i.e. industrial relations, will damage the ability to deliver cost-effective products and services to the customer and also the ability to attract and retain key staff. Any significant damage to corporate reputation will affect the potential for future sales (and hence profit) for a commercial enterprise, leading to a loss of shareholder value. For governments, the consequences of loss of reputation can lead to loss of power at the next election. Failure to manage the environmental impact of operations on neighbourhoods and communities can also significantly damage corporate reputation, and can lead to limitations on how and where to operate.

At the time of writing, London's road transport network is being reported (remember, I am only dealing in perceptions) to be heavily disrupted because of the simultaneous closure of several River Thames crossings for maintenance. This may be the quickest way to complete the work, and may be the best approach to maintain overall traffic flow in London. However, if the communication of this fact to those affected is not effective, it leaves a vacuum in which the media can again emphasise the negative side.

Companies are increasingly required to comply with standards of operation and, again, there is quite a wide range of these. Some are regulatory requirements specific to an individual industry, e.g. airworthiness regulations within the aviation industry. Others are more generally applicable, including quality standards, published by the International Organisation for Standardisation (ISO), and standards for financial reporting and corporate governance. The latter have been progressively developed in recent years after a number of corporate failures such as the Enron scandal. Failure in the area of compliance can damage reputation but can even lead to the inability to trade or operate in certain fields, through the revoking of licences and/or loss of accreditation to ISO or other standards.

Implicit in any concept of a portfolio of activity is the opportunity to spread risk, such that the portfolio can absorb the impact of failure or shortfalls within some of its elements. In other words, any mature approach to portfolio management will allow for and expect some degree of failure within it.

As one illustration of how the spreading of risk across a portfolio works, I recall an anecdote that I first heard in the 1980s, attributed to an approach to new product development by Hewlett Packard (HP). I was told that HP cancelled more than 95% of their new product development projects. Whether apocryphal or not, this story was not trying to imply that this was a sign of failure on HP's part, but rather one of successful innovation. At a time of high innovation, and when it is difficult to predict which of the many new product ideas were going to succeed in advance, the knack is to generate lots of ideas, to spot the failures early enough and to focus effort on the most promising ideas.

In this example, the greater risk for HP was in not innovating enough, which could have led to an inadequate product range in the future. Innovative companies accept that this means some projects get stopped, but this doesn't imply failure to them. Recently I have heard of a couple of innovative companies that regularly celebrate failures, but they are in Brazil and India, not in the UK.

At the corporate level, therefore, the prime drivers of success are value, future capability, reputation and compliance. A contributing factor to success includes how well the corporate body spreads risks across its portfolio of activities. These are the factors that dominate the perception of success or failure at the corporate level.

If we now return to the two main examples already discussed, we can see that the Millennium Dome did not deliver the publicised 'value' of being the centrepiece of the country's millennium celebrations. So, at the corporate level, the failure to deliver the 'Greatest Show on Earth' led to an impact of damage to the government's reputation as well as incurring unplanned costs. However, in the longer term, it did enable the creation of a suitable venue for major events that has become a success as the O2 Arena. This is a corporate level success for the organisation that took over the Dome and also, from the Government's standpoint, for the urban regeneration aspect of the programme. However, the damage to government reputation may have outweighed these achievements.

To some extent, the corporate perspective of Heathrow Terminal 5 is similar. Again, the communication of expectations seems to have contributed to the perceived impact of the failed opening. Those high expectations were set at the corporate level and it is there that the ultimate reputation damage has been felt. Although the programme did experience failure, it may yet recover and ultimately deliver the full vision of success, in terms of the value of the completed re-development programme. Only time will tell whether this also delivers the required future capability.

CONCLUSIONS

None of the projects discussed merit the epithet of 'complete failure'. Aspects of them have failed, and are rich sources of lessons learned, but they are operating and delivering value now. This isn't trying to say that the failures experienced weren't serious and worthy of attention and we can assume that the original investors in each project, especially the Millennium Dome, lost money.

However, to avoid throwing out the baby with the bath-water, we need a broader vocabulary to describe these shortcomings, allowing us to focus on *where* any failure can be attributed, rather than on *whom*. This also leaves more room to discuss where things went right, without appearing to lose sight of the impact of failure.

We do not tend to give the same attention to successes and so do not build a strong knowledge of what went right and why, which means we do not so readily capture the lessons learned from success. It also means we discourage risk-taking in general, with an expectation that it won't work and that failure will be embarrassing. This may be one reason why some of the examples I have discussed included an element of over-optimism in setting expectations. This may have been to overcome some opposition or scepticism in the early stages but it will usually have a bigger rebound effect when the delivered reality does not match the hype.

In the world of projects, programmes and corporations, failure is always a possibility and, as already discussed in this book, the road to success will involve some failure.

The main conclusion arising from this chapter is that we, in the external environment of all this activity, should be resilient enough to deal with failure when it occurs, just as programmes and corporate bodies have to be. We should also be mature enough to understand that failure is not unexpected, especially when we are pushing the boundaries. However, all this relates to dealing with failure when it happens.

Another conclusion is that we all need to be more critically aware of how well projects and programmes are set up and managed before they fail or succeed. Thus we should be more active in expecting and demanding reasonable evidence that projects, programmes and corporate bodies plan for success, while allowing for the possibility of failure. One of the best litmus tests of this approach is to assess how articulate they can be about their risks and how they are managing them.

So, here are some awkward questions we all might ask of any major undertaking before it gets too late:

- *What's your budget for contingency if things go wrong (there often isn't any) and how did you come to that figure?*
- *What will you do if it goes wrong? (Zero points for 'it won't go wrong'.)*
- *What five things could go right and make it easier for you to succeed? (They will probably struggle to think of one.)*

Without good answers to these questions, there is a higher likelihood of project, programme and, ultimately, corporate failure.

References

Association for Project Management (2006). *The APM Body of Knowledge.* *5th Edition*. High Wycombe, UK: Association for Project Management.

Hillson, D. (2004). *Effective Opportunity Management for Projects.* New York, US: Taylor & Francis.

Johnson, G. & Scholes, K. (2002). *Exploring Corporate Strategy*. Harlow, UK: Pearson Education.

MacDonald, M. (1989). *Marketing Plans – How to prepare them and how to use them, Second edition*. Oxford, UK: Heinemann.

Project Management Institute (2008). *A Standard for Program Management, Second edition*. Newtown Square, PA, US: Project Management Institute.

CHAPTER 9:
BUSINESSES MAY FAIL;
DO ENTREPRENEURS?

Iain Scott

A PERSONAL AND PROFESSIONAL VIEW

Failure is not a word beloved by entrepreneurs. Somehow it is not part of the entrepreneurial lexicon. Or, more accurately, entrepreneurs have ceased to use it. Everyone who starts their own business is well aware of the potential for failure. People thinking about starting a business often cite fear of failure as one of their reasons for not doing anything about it. So why is it that when you interview entrepreneurs they become more than a little prickly when you raise the topic of failure?

My original interest and enthusiasm for this topic was aroused by Mitchell Sava's article in the RSA Journal (Spring 2008 issue) entitled 'The Joy of Failure'. There was something that attracted me to the title that was liberating but dangerous. However, as I started to write this chapter I realised that when it came to failure and entrepreneurs, I could not expand on my thoughts without recourse to, and reference to, all the ideas that I have gleaned from my professional career. Attitudes to failure, and changes to those attitudes, could exemplify the changes that can be wrought as an individual moves from thinking about starting a business to being an entrepreneur.

My professional interest comes from the last 18 years of my professional life, and from my business Enterprise Island, during which I have undertaken the research, design and delivery of entrepreneurship programmes. Over the years I have examined how and why people start businesses and analysed how they become entrepreneurs. In the process they learn a very particular response to failure.

This chapter draws on interviews and programmes that I have undertaken involving over a thousand people from places as diverse as Banff and Buchan in North East Scotland to multicultural Bradford via Liverpool, Penzance, Blackpool, Sheffield, Leeds, Croydon, Tynedale, Newcastle and Barnard Castle.

The age range of participants has been wide – from young people aged 16 to mature entrepreneurs of 72 – with backgrounds as diverse as former company directors and the long term unemployed. Between 48-60% of participants in each group were women and we regularly have well over 20% of attendees from black and minority ethnic origins. What unites them is a desire to change their lives through starting a business. And above all what really drives them is the need to learn how to start a business.

I have had unique opportunities to hear about their understanding of what is involved in learning to be an entrepreneur, and how they regard failure at different stages in their entrepreneurial journey.

It is important to make a small digression to stress the learning element here, because without learning there is no change of mindset, and without change of mindset there is no change in attitude to failure. In my experience entrepreneurs are made not born, and anyone can learn how to become an entrepreneur, if they have the desire to do so. As part of Enterprise Island I have been involved in facilitating this process, using an approach which I call Cognitive Business Therapy, a methodology designed to help people become entrepreneurs.

This is a process that helps aspirant entrepreneurs talk about why they want to start a business, what they want from it and how they are going to get there. We provide people with techniques to help them make decisions and analyse risk. Above all we give them small activities or challenges to help them learn by doing. They are then able to reflect on what they have learned and act accordingly. This is completely different from the business planning process which is entirely about the mechanics of business start up. In Cognitive Business Therapy, the journey is personal. The five elements in Cognitive Business Therapy allow individuals the opportunity to:

- Talk things through
- Test themselves
- Test their idea
- Learn by doing
- Get a shock

Any one of the above can be – and is for any particular aspirant entrepreneur – a starting point for change. Entrepreneurship is like learning to swim –

you can't do it by reading a book. Equally you should not dive in at the deep end. The only way is start at the shallow end and build up your confidence, skills and expertise – and learn from other people. Running and starting a business is not for everyone but in my experience anyone can learn. And the only way you can learn to become an entrepreneur is by doing something!

My personal experience of entrepreneurship has developed over many years and my own journey shows my development as an entrepreneur, including my attitude to failure. Initially, I studied history at Glasgow University, then I did a postgraduate teaching qualification. I taught in the public sector for five years, surely a safe option, but then cashed in my pension to start a business. And I must have seemed absolutely nuts to many people. But in doing so, I was no different from many other people taking their first entrepreneurial steps.

At the time I did not ask the question, 'Will I fail?' Instead I asked, 'What if it doesn't work out? What if this happens? What if that happens?' I was always looking for a fallback position. And maybe that's one of the reasons why entrepreneurs rarely talk about failure – because they reflect substantially on what they're doing, and consider many possibilities and alternative directions so that they always have options. And they never close themselves off.

So did my first business fail? Well I would have said probably not. We hit a major problem in the shape of one of the biggest Listeria scares in Britain and my orders dried up as we were moving premises. It was 'unfortunate'. I wouldn't have said it was a failure because the business was actually sold and carries on to this day. For me, and in the opinion of the other entrepreneurs I knew, it was not a failure. How could it be when I had learned so much and acquired so many new skills? Yes, I lost money and yes, we faced a very tough time. But a significant attitudinal and cultural change had occurred within me and there was no question of seeking employment – it was on to the next opportunity. I ended up going back to Glasgow University, working within the Small Business Unit for the following two years, until I'd had enough of academics. Then I went off and started another business that specialised in helping people and communities unlock their enterprise potential.

As part of the research for this chapter I wanted specifically to review attitudes to, and the understanding of, the word failure in relationship to entrepreneurship. I carried out interviews with people who had crossed the Rubicon and started their own businesses, and who had been trading for at least ten years. I then ran a focus group with over thirty MBA students, who were interested in starting a business, but had not yet done so. As a compare and contrast exercise it was revealing, and the results are discussed in the following passages.

Simply put, failure was something only discussed by people who had never had a go at starting their own business.

EXISTING ENTREPRENEURS.

I undertook one-to-one interviews with eight entrepreneurs, and when I asked 'What is your attitude to failure?' I was aware that I'd never used the F word before in any interview with any entrepreneur or anyone who was starting a business. And, significantly, they'd never used the word back. 'What kind of stupid question is that?' was a typical retort.

I was completely and utterly taken aback by the strength of the responses. The tone of the responses ranged from perplexed to virulent. But they were all adamant: failure was not in their vocabulary. What was the problem? Why did the word 'failure' create such a negative attitude in my entrepreneurs? Is it something that they are in denial about? Do they have anti-failure in their DNA?

As I started to probe further and discuss the issue, so the results became more and more fascinating. One of my first interviewees said: 'You don't mean failure – you mean "learning opportunity".' Another entrepreneur said: 'Entrepreneurship is like chemistry – you're always looking for a reaction that will bring you a great result – success, some money, whatever – but you accept that experiments can and will go wrong before you find it.' Two entrepreneurs explained their attitude to the word failure: 'It's not something we would dwell on apart from in the odd dark moment when we went out to start the business, in the early days.'

One interviewee was not only an entrepreneur but a liquidator, and he was quite revealing about all of these responses. He said: 'To use the word "failure" for a business is too simplistic and not appropriate. Using it tells you nothing. Without analysis you won't learn. Without trials you don't grow.'

As my interviews progressed this view was repeated again and again. The term 'failure' was seen as crude and simplistic – used as easy shorthand by those who did not understand the many and various external forces that could bring a business down. And the instincts and attitudes of my entrepreneurs seem to confirm my own wider research. As part of research on why businesses fail, I have identified at least ten factors that could bring a business down. Most are external to the entrepreneur, and are concerned with market forces and the economy.

Entrepreneurs who had experienced setbacks talked freely about their experiences. Some agreed that their businesses failed because they 'overspent'. They were completely honest about it, saying 'we spent too much' or 'we ran out of funds'. Of course, in these times of credit crunch, the concomitant problem may have been that there was not enough investment, or access to it.

Others were not prepared for changes in the markets. Again, these reasons for failure revolved around issues of timing, with sudden black holes opening in an unstable economy, cancelled contracts and consumer jitters.

Sometimes they would say: 'We got the location wrong', which was seen as another learning opportunity. Sometimes they underestimated the complexity of a product, and realised that they needed to reassess their product or process. Even when they said 'We put in a financial controller (for example) who wasn't up to the job', they were not apportioning blame to somebody else, but rather actually recognising that they made a mistake and a bad error of judgement. But they did not consider their judgments or decisions as failure. They could learn from them.

What I noticed from all their answers is that these entrepreneurs have studied and analysed what actually went wrong. I realised that part of the mindset of an entrepreneur is that he or she learns all the time. And they always have. Consider the story of Edison and the light bulb. The story goes that he tried ninety-nine filaments to make a light bulb work and ninety-nine were failures. Was he downhearted? No, he claimed that he now knew ninety-nine filaments that would not work. He could discount them, and move on. He made his failure a learning process .

MBA STUDENTS

Now contrast the responses of existing entrepreneurs with those who are on the other side of the Rubicon – my MBA students.

I set them a list of questions and we discussed them. When asked if they knew what was involved in running a business, 53% said they did, 47% said they did not. 61% felt, however, that they had the skills to start a business. Most also said they would start a business if they had an appropriate idea. So far so positive, and the MBA students seemed to understand in theory many of the factors in business failure that my entrepreneurs had learned the hard way. When I asked them, 'What is stopping you starting in business?', their answers included that they were wary of capital constraints, that they didn't have the right idea or skills to develop their product or were concerned about going it alone without specialist help, particularly in finance. They identified exactly the same risk factors as my active entrepreneurs!

However, when they were asked about taking responsibility for this risk, their confidence seemed to falter. Their main reasons for not starting in business included security in their current job, the opportunity cost (i.e. what would they be giving up, including pension, salary etc.) and family commitments. 65% said that if the risks were removed, they would start their business. When asked what would remove the risks their answers included the ability to start up alongside their current job, a tax free income or grant (!) and support for the transition period from last pay day to first invoice received.

The students wanted someone to take the risks away. They were scared of personal failure, and did not have vision of alternative strategies to minimise this. They cited security in their current job and their guaranteed pay day as reasons for not starting a business. Perhaps they were being prudent, considering their fellows' experiences and the economic times, but without the willingness to jump, and to learn from their own mistakes, it was not surprising that for most of them starting a business had 'simply not crossed their mind'. These students of business did not have the anti–failure gene. And they had not begun their personal journey to entrepreneurship that I believe is essential.

THE ENTREPRENEURIAL MINDSET:
COGNITIVE BUSINESS THERAPY

So what makes an entrepreneur cross their Rubicon? In order for someone to move from employee to entrepreneur there has to be a fundamental change of mindset and the acquisition of new skills. I have always argued that entrepreneurs can be made, and that entrepreneurship is something that can be learned. Entrepreneurship suits some people more than others but everyone can learn enterprising behaviour. And, certainly, entrepreneurship never starts with somebody considering failure; rather, as in my case, considering options. I wondered, 'Can anti-failure DNA be implanted, a kind of enterprise transplant?' I realised that Cognitive Business Therapy did exactly this.

Essentially it separates the business from the individual and is based on the premise that what is good for the individual is not necessarily good for the business, and vice versa. Thus businesses fail, but individual entrepreneurs adapt and learn. So part of the process of learning to be an entrepreneur is to accept challenges as personal development, rather than judge them as personal failures.

The other key element of Cognitive Business Therapy is that 'No business ever started with a plan – it started with a conversation'. One of the reasons few people in the UK start a business is because they do not have an opportunity to talk about their dreams, aspirations, fears and worries. These conversations are not part of our national psyche.

The support mechanisms for businesses in the UK do not encourage this personal reflection. The standard visit to Business Link invariably starts with the question 'Do you have a business plan?' The standard business start up support in the UK (which runs into the multi millions of pounds of Government support) is based around the business idea and then the business plan, not the individual who will risk all to see it through.

To this mix we should also add the media. The version of entrepreneurship we see on TV, in Dragon's Den and its ilk, is all about the idea. Real entrepreneurship is all about the individual. Ironically, the experts who advise and judge are shining exponents of this fact. It could be argued that their success, when contrasted with the aspirant entrepreneurs, makes success seem unattainable and failure a more likely outcome. The inevitable discarding of nine out of ten business ideas and individuals, with the focus on weakness, does nothing to encourage the ordinary, doubt-filled participant (or viewer). And the TV show focuses only on the success of the idea or product, or its failure. The reveal can often show a broken dream – hardly an encouragement to others. Cognitive Business Therapy does not follow this line. Instead, it is all about what the individual wants to do and more importantly why he or she wants to do it. The fundamental point is that you must have a chance to discuss things, including failure. Fear and doubt are very real, but as people work their way through what they are and what they want to do they identify their weaknesses. They also learn how to manage risk.

We have often found that people are more likely to start a business after receiving a shock or surprise. This shock could be a personal or a career shock – something that pushes them out of what they are currently doing. It could be that their wife or husband has run off with somebody else, or that they've been passed over for a job, or that they are unexpectedly fired, or that they discover an idea that they really want to run with. This shock pushes them out of their existing comfort zone and into the area of examining new options, which can include becoming an entrepreneur. That first step on the entrepreneurial journey can sometimes be totally unexpected and there is no room then for thoughts of failure because the individual has already decided to embark on something new. The DNA transplant has taken!

And here we come, perhaps, to the crux of the discussion. Why is it that businesses fail and entrepreneurs adapt? It is because entrepreneurs acknowledge what they're good at doing and what they're bad at doing and they give what they are bad at doing to somebody else to do. How can you possibly fail with that level of self-knowledge? Everyone makes bad decisions and errors and gets the timing wrong – but that's life. Entrepreneurs learn to take a very, very broad view.

I have noticed, also, the absence of guilt or angst among entrepreneurs. They felt that they had done their best, acknowledged their shortcomings, and recognised circumstances beyond their control. If they needed to, they forgave themselves, and moved on. Were that the whole of life could be lived this way! (The flip side, of course, exists; if all the issues have not been considered and thought through and risks assessed, then they pointed out that 'you are a fool and hell mend you'.)

The overall conclusion is that failure is a term used by non-entrepreneurs. It is dismissed by entrepreneurs because it tells you nothing and is a crude and unsatisfactory description. If you are an entrepreneur or want to become one, then you acknowledge that you have to do something. Entrepreneurs are great risk-minimisers – sometimes they get it wrong but that is never failure to them – nor should it be judged as such by those who have not had a go.

ADVICE FOR ENTREPRENEURS

The following advice for would-be entrepreneurs comes from the US via a guest post from New York Entrepreneur Week. This provides a marvellous insight into the workings of the entrepreneurial mind, expressed in language that is totally different from standard MBA-speak.

1. **Ask powerful questions.** When you want results to happen beyond what you normally see or expect, you must reframe your thinking. For example, instead of, 'How can I make money this month?', ask, 'What is the fastest way to generate $10K in the next six weeks?' Your brain goes to work answering that question instead.

2. **Manage limiting beliefs**. These may be your blind spots or you may be well aware of them. First ask others who know you to help you determine what trips you up. For example, you feel you are not a 'numbers person' and therefore cannot keep track of your business' finances. Next, determine workarounds or solutions to that belief.

3. **Shake the cobwebs out.** Often we're deep in our routine. And we cannot fathom breaking out of it to a better or more-efficient way of getting it accomplished. For example, you get a coffee and perform social media posts on Facebook and Twitter for two hours each morning. To break out, assess the impact of your actions to the original purpose for doing your routine.

4. **Build a support team.** This is crucial for really stretching yourself. It is easier for others to see our blind spots that we don't see for ourselves. Create your team of like-minded, committed people that are 'up to' serious things in their lives and they will move mountains for you.

5. **Create your strategy.** Break down your bold, new idea into the three top components. Take your support team and determine fresh and innovative ways to build a powerful set of solutions for achieving what it is you want to achieve. Build a plan around this.

6. **Analyse the Risk.** Compare the *magnitude* of the potential consequences to the *probability* it will happen. Break down your bold new direction into the possible risks involved. Assign potential consequences and probabilities to them. From there create a plan to hedge or protect yourself if you decide to pursue your new, bold idea.

So, any talk of failure is inappropriate for our entrepreneurs, although they rather liked the term 'Glorious Failure'. According to entrepreneurs, failure is for wimps, and the word is only used by people who don't do anything.

© Iain Scott

CHAPTER 10:
FAILURES IN GOVERNMENT ~
'WE DON'T TALK ABOUT FAILURE'

Esmee Wilcox

Failure is such an emotive word. When I first mentioned this project to colleagues you could see the reaction in their faces: we don't talk about failure here. But, despite the silence on the subject, I can think of plenty of examples of things not going as intended – of policy problems that continue to go round and round. We don't articulate these failures together in a way that we can use beyond gaining limited personal insight. We are a long way from having a shared understanding of what we mean by failure, and from being able to value its learning potential in order to change the way we work for the better.

As this collection of essays shows, this picture is not particular to government, but it does emerge very clearly from my experiences of working in central and local government over the last 12 years. In this chapter I want to illustrate some of the particular things about government that drive how failure is perceived, and the consequences of that perception.

First, when we fail in government it can be very difficult to learn from the experience because, for many reasons, we cannot be open about the failure: usually it is a 'sacred' issue, whether because it is a top political priority or relates to a case that would be scrutinised by the media or others, or because achieving success is part of a critical regulatory framework and so has significant consequences for the organisations in question.

It is also often harder to recognise the failure in government because success criteria are not entirely clear or accurate. The distance between decision-makers and the outcomes for citizens and communities (both in central and local government), and the complexity of particular issues that arise in government, mean that success criteria are often emergent rather than fixed from the outset. It can also be difficult to specifically look out for signs of failure where there are, unrealistically, high expectations of success.

DISTANCE OF DECISION-MAKING FROM CITIZENS AND COMMUNITIES

One of the characteristics of government that I have experienced from working in both central and local government, and is increasingly being recognised there, is the way services and policies are organised around professional and organisational boundaries rather than around what makes sense for the citizen or community. This means that decisions are made based on partial information about efficacy. The issue of whether the *individual* professional output works or not is divorced from that of whether the *collection* of professional outputs leads to an effective outcome.

The way we have for so long organised policies and services makes for very strong and varied cultural norms across different services. This gets in the way of bringing together decision-making to focus on the all-round needs of the citizen because that would involve behaving in a way that goes against the organisational norms, in order to collaborate.

At the local level, there are many examples of people trying to shift the barriers between education and health & social care for young people and adults. In response to the Victoria Climbié case, Children's Trusts were created, bringing together social care and education specialists. However, it appears that these structural changes have not enabled the cultural differences to be overcome sufficiently.

In Suffolk, we have run pilots to integrate social care and health provision for adults, based around GP practices. These have proved highly successful in enabling professionals to share experiences and build common approaches that break down barriers, and so to work together to find more effective responses to customers. There are other examples of this working around the country.

Colleagues who work on front-line services tell me that when they are experimenting with integrating services around the customer, the most difficult part is changing the behaviour of the professionals allocating resources. It can be possible to achieve success with small-scale pilots, where you can hand-pick interested professionals and attract investment funding, but there is only so much that you can achieve without changing the whole organisation – the systems and the culture – including being able to scale up.

In Suffolk, the Chief Executives of 30 or so large voluntary, private and public sector organisations are trying to respond to this complex picture by building better relationships amongst themselves to overcome the organisational and professional boundaries that get in the way of running effective services. This collaboration is influenced by whole systems thinking, and it looks very different from traditional command and control models of management. It is about addressing behaviours and organisational cultural norms rather than focusing simply on structural changes. Its origins were partly in the last government's 'Total Place', looking at the total spend in public services in an area and looking for room for streamlining and a better focus on outcomes. It is still carrying favour with the coalition government, for example in the developing concept of community budgeting and, in the emphasis on relationships rather than structural reform, in the focus on collaboration rather than mergers, for example in the Police.

The group has both drawn on examples of and undertaken ethnographic research to try and understand customer behaviour, to get closer to how customers interact with services in order to understand what the outcomes are rather than just looking at outputs of their own services and policies.[1]

Using ethnographic research tools feels very different. It involves taking a big risk in itself, given the investment of resources and the challenge to a system that is concerned with measuring individual outputs rather than outcomes for customers. It's not the only approach, but it is one way of getting much closer to the customer, and making clear and evidence-based decisions about what success and failure look like for that customer.

Another interesting relationship here is the distance between the national and the local within government bodies. The current system of central government tends towards top-down decision-making, in part because, in relating to citizens, it needs to be able to show the ability to control the outputs that will resolve a particular policy problem, and it can't risk

---

1   The 'Mindlab' within the Danish Government has some history of this, and has published case studies and methodologies at www.mind-lab.dk/en

variation in the means where this creates uncertainty about the ability to achieve the outputs.

The problem with centralized decision-making is that it is not able to take sufficient account of the local context, because this would mean different outputs across localities. And so we have national polices that are centrally imposed and are often neither feasible nor desirable within a locality, so they are inherently likely to fail.

The new coalition government is talking a lot about decentralisation and devolution of power and decision-making, but it is too early to tell whether they will implement it to the extent they are talking about. Tactically, it is one way of sweetening the bitter pill of nearly 30% cuts in local government budgets over the next four years: both psychologically in giving people the freedom to act, and practically in taking away some of the costs of reporting to central government. On the positive side, it could force the kind of collaboration that is difficult to enable without a crisis. On the other hand, it will require a very different kind of leadership to prevent organisations holding steadfastly onto their limited remaining resources, when what is required is the sharing of resources, and to ensure more is spent on preventative work rather than reactive and more costly activities.

The Localism Bill, which should receive Royal Assent and become an Act of Parliament during the second half of 2011, is an interesting case in point around the levers we have to create local decision-making. The fact that it is not as prescriptive as other pieces of legislation (see case study on the Sustainable Communities Act below) demonstrates changes in government thinking since the coalition came in. However, a piece of legislation, one of the key levers of central government, is never going to enable the kind of capacity building in local communities that is required to enable people to have the skills and be organised enough to influence local decision-making. There is a conundrum in top-down measures that are about enabling bottom-up influence. They will be about making incremental reforms, where they are designed by the existing institutions. The first wave of reforms will be from within the current centralised and controlling way of thinking, even with the political imperative of the new government. Where we transition into this it may then be possible to create more space for bottom-up influence if, at the same time, community groups are able to organise more.

It does not help that there are strong organisational barriers between central and local government, making it difficult for open dialogue that would allow for more discussion of local variation to happen, whether amongst civil servants and local government officers or politicians. Part of the role of the regional tier of government has been to create links between central and local, but all too often the barriers have been just as strong between regional and central and local, making it difficult to fulfil this function. The stripping away of the regional tier under the coalition government is interesting to watch in terms of this relationship. Will there be more of a requirement for civil servants to work with local government officers to understand the local context? Will they choose to prioritise this when all are undergoing reductions in staff numbers?

The Big Society, despite being about community capacity building and appearing to be a move towards accepting different solutions in different communities, is a top-down instrument. The coalition government has talked about it being deliberately non-prescriptive, with more local control of decision-making. It is very clearly about less state involvement and more local participation in communities. The tension though is that local community development organisations are saying that they need more resources and skills to develop participation in the community, and this is being threatened with both the magnitude of the cuts and in particular the frontloading of the cuts, driven by national politics. The need for innovation to find new ways of organising with less resources is clearly very strong. Will we find ways around this tension between central and local drivers and perspectives? The question remains as to whether the Big Society will become more prescriptive as we see examples of it that are born of the new coalition government and the new political and social and economic reality: will we have to fit with emerging prescriptive criteria in order to access limited resources? Or will it become a movement that shifts central government's ability to exert control over local communities? It may be that we find a different set of levers of influence being deployed.

One of the other characteristics of moving from centralised to localised decision-making is the centralised institutions' ability to initially determine what can and what can't be decided locally. If the Big Society is dependent on more people participating within their communities and being able to make decisions about local issues, what happens when issues that are still determined nationally and are interdependent of devolved issues cannot be influenced locally? What may look like success for devolved and centralised issues may not be the success that communities perceive when they come together. The role of politicians as representatives of their communities will be critical for resolving these issues, but to what extent will they be able to act as representatives of their communities where there is a conflict with their role as legislators or members of the governing body?

So we have seen that the relations between central and local government are significant, but they are only one aspect of how the dialogue over success and failure can become skewed against recognising and acknowledging failure.

LEVEL OF SCRUTINY IN GOVERNMENT: FEAR OF FAILURE

Another particular feature of being in public life is the level of scrutiny by the media, by politicians, by interested individuals and organisations, and by the general public. In itself this is not something that prevents failure as part of innovating, and it actually can be a huge source of innovation: different perspectives being a source for creative thinking and insights into likely impacts (see comments on ethnography above). However, the way it tends to operate at the moment – based on an adversarial system rather than encouraging an open and honest dialogue around the complexities and challenges – means that government responds to the level of scrutiny by acting to prevent publicly acknowledging or allowing for failure.

Many of the issues that we deal with in government carry the risk of great tragedy if something goes wrong. Child protection for example. The reaction to Baby P, and our fear of another failure around child protection, has meant a greater increase in the number of children going into care, in addition to social workers being placed under even more pressure and having to deal with the effects of damage to their professional reputation.

But are we really prepared for the unintended consequences of these decisions? We know that young people leaving care are less likely to find long-term employment. We know that care is very expensive and that local authorities are having to cope with the dramatic budget reductions put in place to manage the public sector debt. We know there is already a shortage of qualified social workers.

Failure in child protection, as with other areas of government, has enormous ramifications. We need to be able to manage these huge risks appropriately.

The fear of failure permeates through everything that goes on in government. It is not just where there are catastrophic consequences that we put lots of control into preventing failure. In many areas of public life, it is the fear of reaction from the media and the public that paralyses our ability to take appropriate risks. You can see it play out in public resignations in response to public failures, without proper debate about whether the failure could have been predicted or whether it was actually a necessary part of finding the answer to difficult problems.

It also came out in the debate around Freedom of Information: that Ministers wanted to be able to have the space to think the impossible, to have ideas about the unfeasible, in order to make system changes, and that scrutiny at this stage of policy development would limit what they could consider. I think the mistrust this debate highlights is partly an effect of the distance and lack of dialogue between policy decisions and citizens that I have talked about above. We need to do things that make the policy process more transparent: if citizens understood it better and felt more able to influence it then they might not be so mistrustful of it and might understand the need to have radical thinking space at times. It is not that people need to participate in everything, but they do need to trust governments to make decisions on their behalf.

The fear of the public outcry has quite a disproportionate effect on our ability to take appropriate risks. It tends to blight organisational decision-making very quickly and for a long time. I started working for the Ministry of Agriculture/Defra a few years after the BSE crisis, and just before the 2001 Foot-and-Mouth Disease outbreak when the merger with the Department of Environment happened – all that was new or born of the Department of Environment appeared to be better, and there was no space to look for and build on the successes from the Ministry of Agriculture's past. I have no doubt that the organisation was in crisis and needed radical reform, but our inability to look intelligently at the past meant that we lost out on insights and learning for the new organisation.

More recently, I have worked for Suffolk County Council, where we have quite an adversarial relationship with the local press. This makes it more difficult to make changes when there is uncertainty over outcome, but, given changing demands on public services, the need for reform is overriding. This is a real issue in an organisation and, arguably, the public sector, when it requires permission from the hierarchy in order to move away from current institutional behaviours, many of which are not appropriate for meeting the new demands on the public sector.

Within democratic organisations, there is also the pressure of a relatively short political cycle. If you have a public failure close to an election, you might not get voted back in. Or if you were to fail publicly, would you have enough time to try again before the next election? What is the temptation to say that the success of a small scale pilot is replicable across the whole county or country, showing how much money you could save for the taxpayer, without having the evidence or knowledge of how to make the pilot work in varied contexts?

This is particularly relevant at the moment, where the coalition government has frontloaded the budget reductions to enable it to start spending again in the run-up to the next national election. Local government elections don't always coincide with general elections, making it difficult to get political buy-in to redesigning services where the benefit has not yet been realised but the investment is being made at election time.

This is one of the critical barriers that I see to innovation in government: that we need to decide to move from pilot to implementation before we understand the nature of the outcomes, because of external pressures. A pilot may not show us the full impact of the intervention, because we may only be looking at a narrow set of measurements, or we may stop a project that needs much longer to show the benefits. We may also not support a project that ends up challenging our view of what success is.

It is also far more complicated to really get to the heart of why something worked where it did. So we try to replicate without knowing what it is that we need to replicate, and we don't take account of how this thing needs to be adapted to the local context in order to work. And then when this happens, the political stakes are too high to enable a withdrawal from huge investments, and again we cannot talk about the failure. Julian Baginni talks about responsible risk-taking in government, including the ability to reverse decisions if they fail[2], which must include not just the political will but the design of the model. The two are interdependent:

2   J.Baginni, (London, 2009).

you cannot build in resilience without support for the skills and resources required for this.

If we can't be open with the public about these kinds of complexities – that we may need very different solutions in different areas, and we shouldn't rush through implementation at scale – how can we have conversations about the very difficult and real issues of reducing the national debt? This is one of the issues that we are concerned with in the County Council I work for, and we recognise that a fundamental shift is required in order to be able to have a really constructive discussion with the whole community – about what is needed to sustain the viability of our communities whilst reducing the national debt.

The changing expectations of and by government to deal with ever more complex issues throw up questions about what the role of government is. I think it needs to be much more about working with citizens as well as across government and public, private and voluntary organisations to facilitate different models of service delivery. This point of view differs from one that sees government's role as being there to provide all the answers. Whilst this latter paternalistic view perpetuates, it is harder for government to work with citizens and the media to resolve issues, particularly where governments have already tried to do so in the past. If we could move to a more realistic expectation – that we need to work together, that governments don't have the answer on their own – then there would be more possibility of open dialogue about the big challenges we face across society. The expanding literature on co-designing public services is quite helpful in thinking about how we can start to do this.[3]

When I worked for a government Minister, one of the things that surprised me most was that dialogue did happen in parliament, when individuals were outside of the main chamber: that it could be pragmatic across party lines at times, and that it could be open about the challenges in the issues rather than reducing the debate down to an either/or view of the world. But I do remember being bitterly disappointed, having listened to a debate in one of the side chambers when scrutinising a parliamentary bill, that despite a varied debate amongst all the party politicians, they proceeded to vote decisively on party lines at the end of it: that openness about the issues did not translate into challenging the institution of the parties.

---

3   For example D. Boyle *et al*, (2010).

Our fear of any failure that could elicit a negative response from a boss is very real in hierarchical organisations. And it means we not only fear failure in the public domain, but failure within the organisations of government. It means we don't talk about any kinds of personal failure, across the mistakes and failures that have been described in Chapter 3, because of the impact on our place in the hierarchy: where your status is derived from success, it is very difficult to talk about failure. It is difficult to be alive to future failure resulting from changes in environmental conditions that have served you well in the past, and where innovations threaten the legitimacy of current institutions it is likely that they will be suppressed.

Our fear of failure stops our personal and organisational development, because we cannot collectively reflect on these experiences. We need to share our experiences to gain new insights and for the motivation to change. The Modernising Rural Delivery example illustrates this (see box). In the literature on learning organisations this concept of collaborative learning is key to organisations being able to adapt and develop.[4]

---

4   For example Jones and Hendry, (1992), Garvin, (1993).

Modernising Rural Delivery: collective learning

The 'Modernising Rural Delivery' programme was the government's response to the Foot-and-Mouth disease crisis and the resulting perception that there was a need for radical reform of the way government related to and delivered services in rural areas. This was a large reform programme that included: passing primary legislation; creating two new arms-length agencies (Natural England and the Commission for Rural Communities) and moving thousands of staff into them; simplifying funding arrangements; and devolving decisions to the regional level.

This was the first time Defra had undertaken such a large change programme, and as such the experience provided opportunities for the individuals and organisations involved to learn on many levels.

The programme came about as a reaction to a crisis, and so the objectives were very politically driven. This meant that, during the implementation from 2004-2006, it was difficult to move away, both publicly and practically, from the original objectives set out in the independent review published in 2003, despite evidence that, in practice, questioned the value of these objectives.

Rather by accident than by design, at the end of the programme, a few staff stayed on to undertake a comprehensive learning exercise, of which I was the lead. A number of staff across the partner organisations participated in a series of interviews, questionnaires, and workshops, leading up to a final workshop with 15 or so senior managers.

What was really constructive was that we created a space where staff could be open about what occurred, and be helped by facilitators and each other in making sense of what happened, and then that they were able to understand and articulate the learning. So, by having the time and space to do this exercise, we created learning from both the failures and the successes of the programme.

> Whilst I was planning the process, one of the non-executive board members told me a story of when he had undertaken an innovative approach to learning within the context of a merger of two global organisations. The learning had such strong conclusions for organisational shift that the Chief Executive of the new organisation could not cope with the implications, and ordered the copies of the published report to be pulped.
>
> On this board member's advice, I tried to get sponsorship at board level to have the report published, because I knew that in order to apply the learning it would require some organisational shift.
>
> Unfortunately, the will wasn't there to publish the report, and it remains on a shelf somewhere. At least the many individuals involved were able to take something from the workshops and I know it has influenced my outlook.

People talk about a no blame culture but my experience is that we are still very fearful of blame and the stigma of failure in government. Perversely, this also means that when we are collectively and individually responsible for failures, all too often we hide them, and so lose the opportunity for learning and not making the same mistakes. Without reflection on the failures it is very difficult to know whether we should have behaved differently, or whether in the circumstances it was the right thing to do.

EXPLOITING OPPORTUNITIES IN A GOVERNMENT CULTURE

It's that feeling of safety and comfort created by a large stable bureaucracy that also means incentives to take a chance on exploiting opportunities are not part of the existing system. So we can choose to ignore the opportunities that we are presented with, and we don't systematically seek out examples of innovation that we could adapt for ourselves. In hierarchies we also become used to not being able to influence decision-making, and fear the consequences of stepping out of institutional norms. So we seek permission before trying something different, which may cost us the opportunity; or we don't do it, out of fear that people above us in the hierarchy will block it.

Government tends to reward individuals that conform, and not the entrepreneurs amongst us. Appraisal systems are based on a rigid view of departmental strategy, rather than understanding that strategy needs to be dynamic. It's far more risky to show how much you have learnt from your failures rather than what you have learnt from your successes.

Attribution Theory[5] also tells us that we tend to think that our own role in success is more reliant on ourselves than any situational factors, so in a different context, if we haven't learnt from the success by interrogating it sufficiently, we may be setting ourselves up for failure the next time.

We need to show how important it is that we create and seize opportunities. We need the 'what if' files: what if we had had the agreement for a university in Suffolk in the 1980s, even though we now have an innovative new one? What if we had the leadership to compel bottom-up models for delivering local services, through the recent Pathfinders for sustainable communities? What if we had the political will to simplify funding not only from national government in the Modernising Rural Delivery programme, but also right through to the sub-regional level as well so it made it easier for communities/small organisations to access it, and flourish?

In government we put layers of bureaucracy around our priorities, as either the answer to questions of accountability or to join up disparate organisations. But our existing behaviours tend to prevent these committees from acting in support of citizens. They remain rigid to objectives that relate to a fixed rather than a dynamic view of the world. And we respond by adapting our communications with them into this rigid view, rather than questioning the view, and in this way we perpetuate the status quo. Consequently professionals can't respond quickly to local needs but end up spending precious resources fixing their requests to meet a distant perception of what needs to happen.

When successful delivery of programmes is part of a key policy that is heavily regulated and linked to organisational status or funding, it is also incredibly difficult to show failure, whether that failure is linked to flaws in the policy or other factors. The consequences of failure are too significant for organisations and professionals to be able to talk about failure.

There are many examples of places where government is trying to move away from this bureaucratic model, but the culture is deeply ingrained, as the case of the Sustainable Communities Act shows (see box).

---

5   Including in D. Halpern, (2010), p 226.

Sustainable Communities Act:
Example of distance and bureaucratic culture in action

The intention behind the Sustainable Communities Act was to provide a legislative framework to encourage innovation and redefine the central/local relationship. The legislation offered legal powers to local bodies to carry out local activities that would impact positively on an area, and were not currently possible within any legislation.

However, the process of implementing the legislation has demonstrated the remaining cultural and knowledge gap between central and local government: namely, that what has currency in central government as a way of handing over power to local communities and encouraging innovation is seen in local government as still being wedded to a very bureaucratic and centralist model.

Local authorities were invited to submit proposals for devolution of powers from central to local government, which would provide a fixed set of powers rather than a general power to act in the best interests of the community. Central government set the Local Government Association (LGA) up to act as an intermediary for the proposals, and the LGA set a number of specific criteria including around ensuring representation in consultation with the community, and in demonstrating impact and sustainability. Given that many local authorities may have taken the view that their existing 'well-being' power gave them a general power of competence to act to ensure the well-being of individuals and communities and so was sufficient to take most action, and that the application process was resource intensive and became very narrowly defined, many local authorities may have been put off applying. The Act was passed in 2007 and the powers were not implemented by the end of that government. However, in December 2010 the coalition government issued decisions on the proposals submitted by local authorities and an action plan for implementation.

What is also interesting about the approach taken in the Act is the centralist approach to innovation. In the last few years a number of initiatives have looked at improving collaboration across tiers of government in a local area. The 'Pathfinder' approach that central government invited local authorities to pilot in the 2006 Local Government White Paper was about genuinely trying to build the right delivery of services in an area from the bottom up. If this had been bolder and ensured more comprehensive participation from authorities and agencies involved, it could have enabled local communities to determine the model of service delivery. If this model required supporting legislation then one single act could have provided powers to enact the model required in each area. In this way, you are starting in the right place for getting services that work locally, you don't distort the activity by narrowing through the legislation, and you can pilot the model without the sense of compulsion to implement new powers.

The disconnect between strategic decision-making and interactions between professional front-line staff and citizens means that we lose opportunities to innovate. So front-line staff aren't aware of the dynamics at the strategic level that may provide them with opportunities, and the 'Chiefs' aren't aware of the reality of the success or failure of the current system.

In the civil service there can be a fairly strong 'need to know' culture, varying in strength between departments. Again, this lack of open communication inhibits insight into opportunities and demand for innovation. I think it also perpetuates the myth of comfort in stability: if I am not being deemed as important enough to know what's really going on, then I won't bother making the extra effort in taking a risk.

The processes government puts in place to access funding reflect the risk aversion and distance between activity/outcomes and decision-making. Audit and regulation of national policies and standards costs local government a significant amount of money, reflecting the national concern about whether or not local government can say they are delivering against the intentions of the national funders. Given the intention to reduce public sector spending to pay back the national debt, we are now seeing a major effort to reduce the spend in these areas.

One of the first things the new coalition government did, in August 2010, was to announce plans to abolish the Audit Commission, and so local government's comprehensive audit assessment. Statutory targets have also now been removed from local government, but the information required to report on these targets still has to be submitted. So although there may be more room for local government to determine what the local standards and activities should be, the cost of reporting is still there. The ability for central government to respond with punitive action, if it is concerned about the information provided, is still there, and this will impact on behaviours in local government.

The coalition government's consultation on these statutory returns of information closed on 4 February 2011. It will be interesting to see what the response is: will this start to enable local authorities to report more intelligently? To be able to employ systems that are focused on being alive to future failure, either from existing customer groups or with new demands arising?

The challenge is to have information that gives real insights into whether or not there are problems with quality, as opposed to information that only creates the perception of high quality and makes it look like we are in control. For example, we appear to maintain good standards by completing 70% of our initial assessments with children within seven days, yet this requirement takes no account of the remaining 30% of cases and so could have intolerable consequences.

Part of the answer may be to develop more collaboration across national government and so to enable local government and the public sector to collaborate in audit and inspection processes: to reduce the burden of regulation, but more importantly to enable it to look at it from a community perspective, where the outcomes of individual public services exist. An approach to the reform of local health services that gives more decision-making about health at a local level would certainly enable health decisions to be aligned with other public services, and is more likely to reduce cost shunting and reduce the spend on reactive services. Public service boards could offer more opportunities for aligning local public services by bringing together the political leadership. However, we should not underestimate how difficult it is to join up government in Whitehall.

Government procurement is another example of where we put lots of control into the system – in this case the system of tendering – which makes us think we're managing the risk involved in working with contractors on major programmes. But what happens when what we actually need is different from what we thought we needed? How can we adapt our commercial relationships to address the need to manage the real risks of failure and the fear and silence that surrounds it?

The constant murmur in government about targets and measurements and devolution and localism masks something more fundamental about how governments know what is successful and what isn't: that what works happens because of a very local interaction between agents; and that complex systems aren't characterised by predictability. If we can appreciate this, we can start to move away from rigid methods of measuring and evaluating, that are not only costly but are also ineffective in assessing what is and what isn't successful.

But in government we want to do things at scale. The public doesn't want a 'postcode lottery', although devolution suggests more political appetite for local variation. Is it through a move to much greater local accountability, with more continuous and constructive scrutiny of decisions, that we could have more scope for new forms of public services to be given sufficient time and resources, to determine their effectiveness over the long term? There are already some innovative examples out there of councillors scrutinising policies by working with service users to peer review their effectiveness, rather than simply debating these in town halls.

So you need political leadership if you are to change the way we go about measuring and targeting in government, to enable experiments to happen that don't have rigid success criteria from the start, and that allow for the answer to emerge from the process. You need people to be comfortable with letting go of the control they normally have, and not to be allowed to respond to 'failure' by putting lots of control back in, but to see it as part of the innovation process.

WHERE NEXT?

So we can see that there are particular forces in government that make it difficult to recognise, understand and/or talk about failure, which means failure is not part of our language and so not an everyday source for innovation to draw on.

Where there are like-minded individuals who are passionate about getting government right, and are prepared to take a risk, I can see we can create opportunities to learn from failure. It's possible to facilitate learning around success and failure with the right motivations and understanding of the need to do so.

Where we are experimenting, we need to understand fully that we are experimenting. We need to put the right boundaries in place and to invest in the right skills, so that we can accept the possibility of failure more readily.

At the same time, we need strategic leadership to foster an understanding that for complex policy problems we cannot readily control the impact of our interventions, meaning we need to allow responses to emerge as part of a process and to differ across a variety of communities and contexts. Within the public sphere we need more focus on adaptive capability, responding to insights as to what is and isn't working.

Leaders in government need to change the dialogue with the public and with the media, so that we understand what we mean by failure and are not afraid of it but are, instead, able to tolerate it. That is, of course, as long as we have put the right resources and skills in place – a task that should not be underestimated – so that we are not making unacceptable mistakes with people's lives.

If we can have this dialogue we can start to create a different conversation with our citizens and communities about what success and failure look like, and how we may fail as we work together to achieve the outcomes we want in our communities.

References

Baggini, J. (2009). 'Mistaking mistakes and the rightness of wrongness'. Online essay. Demos: http://www.demos.co.uk/files/Mistaking_mistakes. pdf?1249924994 [accessed March 2011].

Boyle, D., Coote, A., Sherwood, C., & Slay, J. (2010). 'Right Here, Right Now: Taking Co-Production into the Mainstream'. Nesta, New Economics Foundation.

Halpern, D. (2010). *The Hidden Wealth of Nations*. Cambridge: Polity Press.

Garvin, D. A. (1993). 'Building the Learning Organisation', *Harvard Business Review*, July 1993.

Jones, A. M. and Hendry, C. (1992). *The Learning Organization: A Review of Literature and Practice*. Human Resource Development Partnership.

Phillips, N., Lawrence, T. B. and Hardy, C. (2004). 'Discourse and Institutions', *Academy of Management Review*, 2004, vol. 29, no.4, 635-652.

Stott, M. (ed.) (2011). *The Big Society Challenge*. Cardiff: Keystone Development Trust Publications: http://www.keystonetrust.org.uk/documents/128.pdf [accessed March 2011].

PART 3

CHAPTER 11:
TWENTY-FIRST CENTURY
PERSPECTIVES ON FAILURE

Roxanne Persaud

The Glory of Failure campaign started life as an RSA Fellows project, so naturally it inherits some of the RSA vision and character. In a recent blog post Julian Thompson, RSA Director of Projects, said that at the heart of the Society's argument for a 21st Century enlightenment is the belief that 'we might realise a better world by harnessing the better part of ourselves'. As Fellows we are exhorted to be innovative and to think creatively across a wide range of disciplines. As people we tackle our problems in many different ways. Similarly in both the Glory of Failure campaign and in this book recording our progress to date, we start with personal stories, give perspectives on individual and group behaviours and look towards a society with robust responses to failure and an appetite for experimentation and creation. The Glory of Failure is a spur to push the boundaries of current thinking and practice. Our vision requires a combination of radical thinking, rigorous research, shared reflection and practical recommendations that are then tested and evaluated in real world settings, as illustrated in Part Two of this book.

The aim of the RSA itself, as explained in CEO Matthew Taylor's pamphlet '21st century enlightenment', is: 'enlightenment in the general sense, shedding light on deeply held assumptions so that we can question whether they are up to the challenges posed by the coming century', and the Glory of Failure campaign has the same lofty goal.

Our approach follows the reflexive, holistic behaviour change model championed by the RSA Social Brain project in its second stage report, 'Steer: Mastering our Behaviour through Instinct, Environment and Reason'. We are not only thinking about failure, but also 'thinking about thinking' about failure, and seeking transformational responses at every level. In common with other RSA Fellows in pursuit of 21st Century enlightenment, our objective in the Glory of Failure campaign is to effect a change in how we think of ourselves, as well as a change in our culture, by stimulating innovative responses to shared problems.

At the RSA in 2007, Nassim Nicholas Taleb (an expert in 'risk engineering') shared his first principle for a robust world: 'What is fragile should break early while it is still small. Nothing should ever become too big to fail'. Failure on a large scale appeared on the agenda and quickly became a complicated subject. Inevitably, there is more public discussion about what constitutes 'too big to fail' than about how to mitigate and manage risks for very large organisations and systems. It is hard to comprehend the complexity of the problem or the tipping point when something becomes 'too big to fail'. This phrase is described in *Wikipedia* as 'a term of art in regulation and public policy that refers to businesses dealing with market complications related to moral hazard, economic specialisation and monetary theory'. These three market complications have each been subject to extensive analysis, but as yet there has been little published work examining the distinctive 'typology of failure' for businesses being 'too big to fail'. It is this typology and its application that we have explored in *The Failure Files*.

FAILURE IS NATURAL

In this chapter I compare the insights contained in the various perspectives on failure described in Part Two to the vision in Part One. The aim is to draw out common threads from these chapters showing where the failure principles are generic, and also point out any variations that are domain-specific. It seems appropriate to start with a quick reminder of the scene-setting in the first two chapters which form Part One.

In Chapter 1 Mitchell Sava set out the underlying problem that we seek to explore: 'a pervasive fear of failure'. This fear is deep-rooted in our collective and individual psyches, as well as in our bodies. 21st Century thinker and marketing expert Seth Godin claims that fear is the dominant emotion of our lives because our brains have evolved to see failure as a matter of life-or-death. He calls this the 'lizard brain', based on the 'reptilian brain' described by Paul MacLean in the 1970s. (MacLean's work on the Triune Brain set out how basic survival instincts rooted in this part of our brains control our behaviour and influence the decisions we make.)

Fear of failure is closely related to fear of criticism and fear of rejection, both of which underpin the negative characteristics of failure listed by David Hillson in Chapter 2. Even those characteristics that seem positive can be problematic – for example, failure may be fun and stimulating, but too much fun is distracting, and over-stimulation can be exhausting.

Sometimes we find ourselves thrust into the Failure Zone, from which it can be painfully hard to escape. It may be too much for us to hold back the forces of fear, but we can reframe failure as learning and practise the Three Ms of resilience: *Mindset* towards failure (rather than away from it), *Minimising* its occurrence and *Maximising* its value. We can all learn to overcome our fear of failure, to recognise and respond to failure skilfully, and to build our resilience and resistance to the demands of the lizard brain.

We learnt in Chapter 2 that resilience is the central strategy for responding appropriately to failure and for avoiding catastrophic damage to ourselves, our organisations and society. Avoiding failure is itself considered a failing strategy, because failure is inevitable and universal. Our capacity to adapt to shocks and changing circumstances is fundamental to our survival according to the natural laws of competition. The trick is to develop a mindset that helps us recognise different dimensions of failure, to embrace those that help us learn and become resilient, while minimising those that extend the boundaries of the Failure Zone beyond our abilities to cope. In physics, resilience is related to elasticity; it's the property of a material that can return to its original shape or position after deformation. Complex organisations and societies can further benefit from this link between the concept of resilience and notions of elasticity. What is also without doubt is that resilience at all levels of scale and complexity is based on the human quality of adapting flexibly to the needs of complex situations. This flexibility is the key to responding to failure at personal, organisational and societal levels.

The pervasive fear of failure, highlighted by Mitch Sava in Chapter 1 as the core problem, can be illustrated by a seemingly unrelated question: *Why is failure like underwear?* The answer: *It's not supposed to be seen in public.* Just as we expect people to be discreet about their underwear, we expect people to be quiet about their failures and we are squeamish when serious failings are exposed. We all know that underwear is worn by everyone, but revealing our underwear invites a level of intimacy which can be unsettling, and of course public nakedness is well beyond society's expectations for most of us. There is a taboo around underwear which advertisers tap into when they use images that push the boundaries of convention. Revealing underwear is a bit shocking, titillating or exposing. The lizard brain stimulates similar excited reactions when our failings are exposed.

The inspiration for this underwear comparison came from two recent internet Facebook campaigns: the Pink Chaddi (2009) and the 'Bra Colour' meme (2010). Both exploited the relatively light shock value of exposing underwear in order to shed light on a deeper issue. In February 2009, to oppose a distressing trend of violence against women going to pubs or wearing clothes considered 'unsuitable', the Bangalore-based Alternative Law Forum (ALF) launched a satirical campaign to support India's 'Pubgoing Loose and Forward Women'. The Pink Chaddi Campaign on Facebook asked women to send pink chaddis (a slang word for underpants or boxer shorts) to the ALF to forward to one of the leading groups of aggressors, the Shri Ram Sene. The campaign attracted lots of media and political attention, which contributed to more than 100 Shri Ram Sene members being detained in custody after they had made threats to couples intending to publicly celebrate Valentine's Day.

In January 2010, the question 'What colour is your bra?' spread quickly around Facebook networks, prompting women to publicise the answer in their status update. The origins of the 'Bra Colour' meme are a matter of speculation, and its purpose is still unclear, yet it demonstrates the willingness of people to expose themselves to social failure in small ways in furtherance of a cause (or just for fun). Both these campaigns were relatively low cost, intriguing, liberating and fun – all of which are also attributes of the Glory of Failure project. We too recognise that there are 21st Century opportunities to reduce the costs of failure, to support each other through the Failure Zone and to play with new ways to challenge the taboo surrounding failure.

Another important concept outlined in Part One of *The Failure Files* is the seeming paradox that success and failure are necessary components of each other. This is captured through notions of integration and balance represented by the Taijitu symbol discussed in Chapter 2 (see Figure 2-3). The light and dark aspects of failure/success are also reflected in the ten characteristics, which are themselves shades of grey (see Figure 11-1). For each, there is a repeating pattern of mutual synergies between positive and negative. The yin in the yang is the sand in the oyster, the dark in the light. *The Failure Files'* perspectives demonstrate this success-failure duality by exploring how in people failure stimulates creativity, in organisations it supports innovation, and in society it leads to progress.

Figure 11-1: Expanded Taijitu symbol showing 'light and dark' failure characteristics

In Summer 2007, *Business Week* small business advisor Doug Hall wrote an article extolling the values of a 'Fail Fast' approach to growth, stating that 'The development of a successful new product, service, or business is often the result of lots of learning from lots of failures. The key is to fail fast and fail cheap.' Failure is the crucible of innovation. 'Fail Fast' requires rapid take-up of new ideas, methods and activities, and the speedy abandonment of those that show no promise. Failure and innovation are both required to push us and our organisations through the Success-Failure Ecocycle described by David Hillson in Chapter 2. But innovation is difficult at every level and becomes more complex the more people and infrastructure are involved. 'Fail Fast' requires strong resilience and, crucially, it relies on the directional nature of failure to inform quick success. If you fail fast, you can leave time to figure out how to succeed. This concept underlies many of the perspectives found in Part Two of *The Failure Files*.

EXPLORERS IN THE INNOVATION SUCCESS ZONE

In *The Failure Files* we see how people experience shocks and change, and how they regard failure differently at different stages of life. Similarly, organisations at different levels of complexity or maturity change in their responses to failure. The glory in our campaign title might be a good way of expressing this common changing approach to failure, by increasingly viewing it as discovery, by finding some joy in learning from failure, or feeling a sense of glory or transformation when breaking new ground in what David Hillson calls the Innovation Success Zone (see Figure 2-2). In this zone we become explorers, striving beyond the limits of failures experienced by others. Iain Scott introduces this metaphor in Chapter 9 where he describes the attitude of entrepreneurs as artists and explorers. These are the people who lead us into unfamiliar territory, knowing that they are on a journey and will inevitably encounter setbacks.

The early contributions to Part Two of this book are broadly concerned with individual perspectives. These start in Chapter 3 with Marilyn Fryer, who supports our call for intrepid explorers, describing the greatest failure as 'inaction in the face of opportunity, failure to engage in living and find out what might be'. Marilyn identifies curiosity and the ability to seek and use feedback as intrinsic qualities for learning and discovery; these are common characteristics of explorers through the ages.

Our individual responses to failure must be set in the context of societal change otherwise we will find our organisations and society stagnating or becoming irrelevant, which, as Chapter 4 points out, is another type of failure. Cliff Leach's conclusions underline the seeds of failure in success: the need for flexibility and responsiveness both in the definition of success and of our striving towards it. In identifying success as a capacity of a society or social system he gives us a tool for reframing failure as 'learning' for individuals and organisations too. Success is dependent upon responding to context adequately and acceptably, so our challenge is also to reach an awareness and understanding of context, especially during times of growth.

The 'individual' theme is continued in Chapter 5 on educational failure. Susan Greenberg emphasises the importance of characteristics typical of explorers and innovators when she says '... any new idea, explored in turn, will not only do away with the difficulty, but will soon produce a whole new set of problems, mistakes and doubts; *and this is as it should be*'. There is no clear distinction between explorer and mapmaker here. Failure is universal and we are all innovators.

We also encounter the boundary between individual and societal failure in Chapter 6 where Robert Morrall and Kirsty Patterson show how feelings of victimhood and futility may be forms of self defence against failure. Like many of the other perspectives, they demonstrate that failure should be seen as an inevitable step on the road to success, not a punishment for seeking improvement. There is no expertise without failure – our novice stage in any endeavour allows us to innovate. And yet we routinely keep the spotlight firmly fixed on the star performers while leaving the benefits of failure in the shadows.

Reflective practice is another common theme in *The Failure Files*, as an essential response to failure. The stigma of failure means it is uncomfortable for us to look in the mirror even in private, and painful to expose our efforts to public scrutiny or judgement. Uncomplimentary feedback is another negative consequence of failure, and a painful aspect that we are keen to avoid. Yet we know that painful self-awareness and the ability to set ourselves in context is integral to improvement, giving the truth to another popular saying, 'No pain, no gain'.

These personal and psychological perspectives offer some deep analysis of motivation and learning in relation to failure, especially the importance of our emotional state in framing our responses. The theme of painful self-awareness returns in Chapter 7, in which Christopher Knell draws on personal life events to conclude that experiencing failure affects our capacity in the future as well as the immediate aftermath. It also adds another dimension to our ability to expand our Comfort Success Zone (see Figure 2-1). What is clearly outside our control is the immediate impact of catastrophic events, and we should recognise the possibility of minimising the longer-term consequences even though our capability to deal with them is set back. Some people will consider their problems as a consequence of an earlier life event, which is justifiable. And yet context is paramount; recognising that experiencing failure creates an ongoing predisposition to failure is a vital step towards reframing and de-stigmatising failure. As Christopher points out, 'there is no rule book', so why do we behave as if there is?

For many people failure is a frightening word, used in dark moments. Several chapter authors have called it the 'F-word' even as they attempt to illuminate it. This is not only true of individuals facing failure. Other perspectives in Part Two reveal the same view. For example, Chapter 8 provides signposts to the factors that dominate negative perceptions on the road to project, programme and corporate success or failure. Stephen Charters also notes that media perceptions and our own reporting of failure obscure the information we need to learn from failure and take direction from it. For some organisations, fear of failure might be part of the psychology or emotional state. Chapter 9 tells us that the F-word is not part of entrepreneurial language in Iain Scott's experience, and that the media spotlight reinforces the idea of failure as a verdict rather than an opportunity for learning and a doorway to success. In Chapter 10, Esmee Wilcox suggests that in the public sector there is strong anxiety about admitting failure (or even discussing it), and fear of the consequences of scrutiny or harsh judgement in a complex media-sensitive environment where measures of success can be unrealistic. Even within the public sector the dialogue between central and local government is 'skewed'.

Perhaps a good way to close this review of the various failure perspectives described in Part Two is to take the approach recommended by Stephen Charters in Chapter 8. Are we serious about developing 'a mature attitude to failure in general', and are we prepared to share our perspectives individually, in our organisations and in wider society? Central to developing a sophisticated, stigma-busting approach to failure is the understanding that perceptions, perspectives and context are paramount.

CLOSING CONVERSATION

Failure is without doubt a 21st Century subject, and examples abound. In Spring 2010, *Time Magazine* put 'freedom to fail' at number six of ten important trends of the new decade. The editorial called for us to remember our lessons from past failures as the key to avoid repeating mistakes, which we might characterise as getting stuck in the Failure Zone. Responses and resilience are at the heart of another contemporary concept of 'failing badly'. This comes from systems and network security analysis, and was popularised by security guru Bruce Schneier. 'Failing badly' goes hand-in-hand with 'failing better' for Schneier, who believes that systems that fail badly are brittle, and systems that fail well are resilient. As we have seen throughout *The Failure Files*, echoes of these systems thinking principles can be applied on the human level. In particular, the importance of personal flexibility – 'bounce-back-ability' – has been emphasised as vital to our ability to explore the benefits and opportunities that failure presents. More colloquially, especially on the internet, there appears to be no shortage of people willing to share (sometimes sensationally) their mistakes and experiences of failure and crises. Perhaps reflecting its surging influence on online communication, the word 'fail' was voted 'Word of the Decade' in 2009 by the American Dialect Society.

Failure events and their consequences are often clear and measurable. Our capabilities and responses are not. In reflecting on these difficult and challenging issues, *The Failure Files* presents us with a wide range of provocative statements and questions. Reflection gives us options, and looking back at the bumps in the road helps us recognise and anticipate what might be around the next bend. This offers an essential practice for reducing the potentially debilitating effects of failure on our lives and livelihoods. We can all do this. Learning is not at all automatic, and productive reflection requires a thorough and systematic examination of our failures. We all have been explorers, making our path through life on the stepping-stones of more failures than we care to remember.

Most people would say that failure is to be avoided. Nevertheless the overarching contention of *The Failure Files* (and of the wider Glory of Failure campaign) is that failure is also something to be embraced. We are making our first public steps in a learning process that breaks the taboos of failure, and seeking to change the terms of engagement with failure in different fields. We are not flinching from the hard questions or from reflecting on our ability to answer them. This book is a step on our journey and every contributor stands ready to continue this conversation with every reader.

You can begin your own transformation by starting a Glory of Failure conversation within your circle of friends and colleagues. To help you and them address failure wherever you encounter it, you might consider some of these questions drawn from *The Failure Files*:

- Why is fear of failure a significant barrier to social progress?
- How confident can we be that we have enough information to take the next steps through the Failure Zone towards innovation and success?
- Who is the best judge of your failure?
- How much do you think about contingency in your planning and how you measure and mitigate it?
- Which criteria can we use to evaluate the success or failure of our society?

- What happens if we follow the creative insights from playful and reflective practices?
- Are the consequences of failure too significant to be able to talk about it?
- If you knew you were going to fail, would you do things differently?

Since Mitchell Sava first wrote about the 'Joy of Failure' in the RSA Journal in Spring April 2008, a range of leaders from diverse fields have explored ways to understand what it might mean to fail gloriously. This led to the Failure Colloquium in September 2009 where speakers shared their ideas and insights on failure in a variety of settings. Those present realised they were hearing a message that was unique and special and from that realisation *The Failure Files* book became our focus for 2010. It is a sign of the times that we draw vitality from talking and thinking about failure, and we think others will be similarly enlivened during our 2011 series of seminars around the UK.

The Glory of Failure is a forum for musings, analysis and transformation to a world where we can create, innovate and thrive free from the stigma of failure. We invite you to explore and promote the benefits of failure within organisations, for individuals and society. Find out more on our website www.glory-of-failure.org.

References

Grist, M. (2010). 'Steer: Mastering our behaviour through instinct, environment and reason'. RSA Social Brain Project, RSA. Available online at: http://www.thersa.org/projects/social-brain/reports/steer-the-report (accessed March 2011).

MacLean P. D. (1974). *Triune conception of the brain and behaviour (The Clarence M. Hincks memorial lectures)*. Toronto, Canada: University of Toronto Press.

McArdle, M. (2010). 'In Defense of Failure'. Time Magazine online: http://205.188.238.181/time/specials/packages/article/0,28804,19711 (accessed March 2011).

Schneier, B. (2003). *Beyond Fear: Thinking sensibly about security in an uncertain world*. New York: Springer-Verlag.

Taleb, N. N. 'The Black Swan – Thinking the impossible?' lecture given at the RSA 1 May 2007. An audio recording of the lecture is available online at: http://www.thersa.org/events/audio-and-past-events/2007/the-black-swan--thinking-the-impossible (accessed March 2011).

Taylor, M. (2010). '21st Century Enlightenment'. RSA. Available online at: http://www.thersa.org/about-us/rsa-pamphlets/21st-century-enlightenment (accessed March 2011).

Thompson, J. 'Edging towards enlightenment'. RSA. Comment blog posted 25 June, 2010. Available online at: http://comment.rsablogs.org.uk/2010/06/25/edging-enlightenment/ (accessed March 2011).

REFERENCES AND FURTHER READING

ONLINE REFERENCES

BAGGINI, J. 2009. Making mistakes and the rightness of wrongness. http://www.demos.co.uk/publications/mistaking-mistakes. Demos.

CADDELL, J. The Mistake podcast. *On innovation, leadership, and understanding customers.* Available from: http://caddellinsightgroup.com/blog2

DIXIT, J. Jul 2009. The Failure Interview Series – 9 prominent people talk about their failures. *Psychology Today: Brainstorm* [Online]. Available from: http://www.psychologytoday.com/blog/brainstorm/200907/the-failure-interview-series

MARKS, J. 2009. Failure as a Strategy – Observations from Nicolas Nova. Vimeo. Available from: http://www.vimeo.com/4250160

MCARDLE, M. 2010. In Defense of Failure. *TIME* [Online]. Available: http://www.time.com/time/specials/packages/article/0,28804,1971133_1971110_1971107,00.html

MCGREGOR, J., SYMONDS, W. C., FOUST, D., BRADY, D. & HERBST, M. 2006. How Failure Breeds Success. *Business Week* [Online]. Available: http://www.businessweek.com/magazine/content/06_28/b3992001.htm

WHITTEMORE, N. January 12 2010. Stay Hungry, Stay Foolish: What 'Failure' Really Means. *Social Entrepreneurship* [Online]. Available from: https://news.change.org/stories/stay-hungry-stay-foolish-what-failure-really-means

[All accessed March 2011.]

BOOKS

ARIELY, D. (2008). *Predictably irrational: The hidden forces that shape our decisions.* Harper New York.

BERNS, G. (2008). *Iconoclast: a neuroscientist reveals how to think differently.* Harvard Business School Press.

DE BOTTON, A. (2004). *Status anxiety.* London: Hamish Hamilton.

BURCHELL, B. & HUGHES, A. (2006). *The stigma of failure: An international comparison of failure tolerance and second chancing.* University of Cambridge, Centre for Business Research.

DIAMOND, J. (2006). *Collapse: How societies choose to fail or succeed*. Penguin Group USA.

MORDAUNT, J. (2004). 'What should happen when governance fails?' *Developing an Integrated Strategy for the Voluntary and Community Sector: volume of evidence.* Newcastle upon Tyne, UK: The Foundation for Good Governance.

ORMEROD, P. (2007). *Why most things fail: Evolution, extinction and economics.* Wiley.

PETROSKI, H. (2006). *Success through failure: the paradox of design.* Princeton University Press.

TAYLOR, S., ROGERS, J. & STOREY, J. (2005). 'Evolution and experimentation: the Barclays University case'. *In:* PATON, R., PETERS, G., STOREY, J. & TAYLOR, S. (eds.) *Handbook of corporate university development: managing strategic learning initiatives in the public and private domains.* London, UK: Gower Publishing.

TAYLOR, S., THORPE, R. & SHAW, S. (2003). 'Neither market failure nor customer ignorance: the organizational limitations of employee training and development'. *In:* STEWART, J. & BEAVER, G. (eds.) *Human resource development in small organizations: research and practice.* London, UK: Routledge.

VOLTAIRE, F. & VOLTAIRE (1759). *Candide, or, Optimism.* Wordsworth.

ZANDER, B. & ZANDER, R. (2000). 'Giving an A: Rejecting the Success/Failure paradigm and practicing the Art of Possibility'. *The Art of Possibility–Transforming Personal and Professional Life.* Boston, MA: Harvard Business School Press.

ARTICLES

ABELE, A. E., RUPPRECHT, T. & WOJCISZKE, B. (2008). 'The influence of success and failure experiences on agency'. *European Journal of Social Psychology,* 38.

ALTERMATT, E. R. & BROADY, E. F. (2009). 'Coping with Achievement-Related Failure: An Examination of Conversations between Friends'. *Merrill Palmer Quarterly,* 55.

AMIR, D. (2009). 'On the lyricism of failure'. *Journal of Poetry Therapy,* 22.

ANHEIER, H. K. (1996). 'Organizational failures and bankruptcies: What are the issues?' *American Behavioral Scientist,* 39, 950.

CARDON, M., STEVENS, C. & POTTER, D. (2009). 'Misfortunes or mistakes? Cultural sensemaking of entrepreneurial failure'. *Journal of Business Venturing.*

CENTOLA, D. (2009). 'Failure in Complex Social Networks'. *Journal of Mathematical Sociology,* 33.

COELHO, P. & MCCLURE, J. (2005). 'Learning from Failure'. *Mid-American Journal of Business,* 1, 13–20.

DRUCKER, P. (2002). 'The discipline of innovation'. *Harvard Business Review,* 80, 95-104.

EITEL, D. (2004). 'The Dynamics of Chronic Failure: A Longitudinal Study'. *Public Money and Management,* 24.

ELLIOT, A. J. & THRASH, T. M. (2004). T'he Intergenerational Transmission of Fear of Failure'. *Personality and Social Psychology Bulletin,* 30.

FARSON, R. & KEYES, R. (2002). 'The Failure-Tolerant Leader'. *Harvard Business Review,* 80, 64-71.

GLĂVAN, B. (2008). 'Coordination Failures, Cluster Theory, and Entrepreneurship: A Critical View'. *Quarterly Journal of Austrian Economics,* 11.

HIGHHOUSE, S. (2007). 'Applications of Organizational Psychology: Learning Through Failure or Failure to Learn?' *Historical perspectives in industrial and organizational psychology,* 331–352.

HOGARTH, R. & KARELAIA, N. (2008). 'Entrepreneurial Success and Failure. Working Papers' (Universitat Pompeu Fabra. Departamento de Economía y Empresa), 1.

KIM, J. & MINER, A. (2007). 'Vicarious learning from the failures and near-failures of others: Evidence from the US commercial banking industry'. *Academy of Management Journal,* 50, 687.

KNOTT, A. M. & POSEN, H. E. (2005). 'Is failure good?' *Strategic Management Journal,* 26.

MAY, P. (2008). 'Policy learning and failure'. *Journal of Public Policy,* 12, 331-354.

MICHAEL, S. & COMBS, J. (2008). 'Entrepreneurial Failure: The Case of Franchisees'. *Journal of Small Business Management,* 46.

MOORE, J. M. (2009). 'Penal reform: a history of failure'. *CJM – Criminal Justice Matters,* 0.

MORDAUNT, J. & CORNFORTH, C. (2004). 'The role of boards in the failure and turnaround of non-profit organizations'. *Public Money and Management,* 24, 227-234.

OWEN, T. B. (2009). 'Failure Means Opportunities'. *Legal Information Management,* 9.

POTTS, J. (2009). 'The innovation deficit in public services: The curious problem of too much efficiency and not enough waste and failure'. *Innovation: Management, Policy & Practice,* 11, 34-43.

PROBST, G. & BORZILLO, S. (2008). 'Why communities of practice succeed and why they fail'. *European Management Journal, 26.*

ROMO, F. P. & ANHEIER, H. K. 1996. Success and failure in institutional development: A network approach. *American Behavioral Scientist, 39,* 1057.

ROSS, D. (2006). 'Evolutionary game theory and the normative theory of institutional design: Binmore and behavioral economics.' *Politics Philosophy Economics, 5,* 51-79.

SAMUELS, L., JOSHI, M. & DEMORY, Y. (2008). 'Entrepreneurial failure and discrimination: lessons for small service firms'. *Service Industries Journal, 28.*

SCHRENKER, R. (2007). 'Learning from failure: The teachings of Petroski'. *Journal Information, 41.*

SEANOR, P. & MEATON, J. (2008). 'Learning from failure, ambiguity and trust in social enterprise'. *Social Enterprise Journal, 4,* 24-40.

SHAFFER, S. (2008). 'Value-neutral tradeoffs between failure risk and growth'. *Applied Financial Economics Letters, 4.*

SHEPHERD, D. A., COVIN, J. G. & KURATKO, D. F. (2009). 'Project failure from corporate entrepreneurship: Managing the grief process'. *Journal of Business Venturing, 24.*

STOREY, J. & BARNETT, E. (2000). 'Knowledge management initiatives: learning from failure'. *Journal of Knowledge Management, 4,* 145-156.

WALSHE, K., HARVEY, G., HYDE, P. & PANDIT, N. (2004). 'Organizational Failure and Turnaround: Lessons for Public Services from the For-Profit Sector'. *Public Money and Management, 24.*

WILBY, P. (2008). 'The price of failure'. *New Statesman, 0.*

WOOD, M. S. & PEARSON, J. M. (2009). 'Taken on Faith? The Impact of Uncertainty, Knowledge Relatedness, and Richness of Information on Entrepreneurial Opportunity Exploitation'. *Journal of Leadership and Organizational Studies, 16,* 117-130.

ZERBE, R. O. & MCCURDY, H. E. (1999). 'The failure of market failure'. *Journal of Policy Analysis and Management, 18.*

ZUCKERMAN, M. (2006). 'Attribution of success and failure revisited, or: The motivational bias is alive and well in attribution theory'. *Journal of Personality, 47,* 245-287.

CONTRIBUTOR BIOGRAPHIES

Steve Charters MSc CEng MBCS MAPM is an independent consultant in risk, project and business change management. His background is in Operational Research and he has had a long career in practising change management in large UK companies. He is particularly interested in the effective use of Information Technology and in improving people's attitude to risk.

Dr Marilyn Fryer BA(Hons) GradCertEd C.Psychol. CSci. AFBPsS FRSA is Managing Director of The Creativity Centre Ltd and co-founder of the Creativity Centre Educational Trust. She specialises in human and organisational psychology, innovation, and creativity in its widest sense. Her work involves consultancy, research, speaking and publishing – in the United States, Mexico, Japan, Malaysia, Eastern and Western Europe and Africa, for example. Marilyn especially enjoys writing and is a member of the Society of Authors.

Susan Greenberg FRSA is a senior lecturer in creative writing at Roehampton University, London, following a long career as a reporter, writer and editor. She has special interests in narrative journalism and internet publishing, and is carrying out research on 'editing' at University College London's Department of Information Studies.

Dr David Hillson FRSA HonFAPM FIRM FCMI CMgr is The Risk Doctor, with an international reputation as a leading thinker and expert practitioner in risk management. David writes and speaks widely on the topic, and consults across the globe specialising in both strategic and tactical risk management, with a particular interest in risk psychology.

Jonathan Jewell RN PGCE Dip.IoD FCMI FRSA is Executive Chair of and Principal Consultant for Chargé de mission Limited, a recovery and renewal consultancy to the Third Sector. He has failed in practically every field of human endeavour but is still with us. Jonathan has extensive experience both in the boardroom as a trustee and director, and frontline as a nurse and educator amidst a range of other roles. He has a special interest in upstream influences on failure, including the role of education.

Christopher Knell FRSA MIOD MAAT is a social entrepreneur and accountant with considerable experience of management roles in the public sector and directorship roles in the charitable sector. He also complements his experience in these fields with private sector exposure through his role as a founding committee member of the London Institute of Directors Young Directors Forum.

Cliff Leach FRSA is presently Director of The Project Factory, a UK high security IT consultancy. He is also co-founder of the GOA Project and is involved in charity through The Backup Trust. Cliff is founder of a number of IT businesses including Chatsfield Technologies and Interaxion. He was previously Technical and Strategy Director for AT&T, and held a number of senior technology posts in the UK and USA. Cliff has been a paraplegic since a road accident in 1977 ended his career with the RAF. He is married, lives in Salisbury and has 4 sons.

Robert Morrall MBA MTS FRSA is a social entrepreneur working with socially marginalised groups and the Criminal Justice System. His work has been recognised by the BITC 'Seiff Award' and the EEDA award for 'Outstanding Contribution to ESF'. Robert is a member of the Ministry of Justice Reducing Re-offending 3rd Sector Advisory Board, co-ordinates the EU Learned Helplessness and Failure network and is a regular speaker on social inclusion, labour market issues and the rehabilitation of offenders.

Kirsty Patterson started working with ex-offenders, long-term unemployed and lone parents through the ESF Funded CEMENT Project in January 2005. Now working for Cementafuture, Kirsty supports the resettlement of offenders and the reduction of re-offending in the community through social incubation interventions. Kirsty is a member of the Hertfordshire Offender Skills and Employment Forum, HACRO (Hertfordshire Association for the Care and Resettlement of Offenders) and Pictora. Kirsty participates in the EU Learned Helplessness and Failure network.

Roxanne Persaud MSc LFRSA is an independent consultant to social start-ups, working on capacity building and enterprise development in Third Sector organisations. Her background in charity management in the UK, overseas and online supports specialisms in participative governance and evaluation, digital engagement and organisation learning. She is currently on the NCVO sponsored Leadership 20:20 Commission working to create a network of emerging leaders in Civil Society. Roxanne's sociopreneurial commentaries can be found on twitter @commutiny.

Mitchell Sava MPA MSc FRSA MIOD is an entrepreneur and innovation evangelist. He currently leads an internet startup, polyWonk. He also advises various agencies on why innovation is more than a buzzword, and how to best unleash the nation's innovative potential. Mitch has worked across business, academia, and government, and is fascinated by innovative entrepreneurs and what drives them. He has experienced his share of failure, to which his very patient wife will attest.

Iain Scott MA(Hons) FRSA is a leading specialist in how people learn to become entrepreneurs. For over eighteen years his company Enterprise Island and his process Cognitive Business Therapy has been used to stimulate enterprise activity in communities across the UK, including both advantaged and disadvantaged. His recent work has focused on how skilled professionals can move from the mindset of an employee to an entrepreneur.

Esmee Wilcox MA MCMI FRSA is a policy and organisational development manager, currently working in local government. Her experience ranges from working with Ministers and Special Advisers in reactive political environments to developing cross-government strategies and implementing large-scale change programmes. She has worked in a number of central government departments and agencies, including the Prime Minister's Strategy Unit.

INDEX

Lightning Source UK Ltd.
Milton Keynes UK
01 April 2011
170217UK00001B/26/P